## WHAT PEOPLE ARE SAYING ABOUT
## 2000 MILES ON WISDOM

"Need an inspiring story to renew your commitment to success? Look no further than Jim Serger's 2000 Miles on Wisdom, with lessons on leadership and delivering the best to everyone – customers, colleagues, relatives, and friends – in your life."
Marshall Goldsmith -million-selling author of the New York Times bestsellers, MOJO and What Got You Here Won't Get You There

"Jim Serger is an evangelist for bicycling and for superior customer service. 2000 Miles on Wisdom brings these two worlds together in purpose and in joy. Join Jim for the ride of his lifetime. This is a true story that will uplift you at every turn and show you how to make our world a better place every day."
Ron Kaufman -New York Times bestselling author, Uplifting Service

"Customer service excellence, a personal journey of determination, and a passion for "making a difference" are at the center of Jim Serger Jr's analytic and personal work. Jim's book demonstrates how a customer-experience business (in his case a bicycle shop) can enliven the passion of customers, produce transformation for those it serves, and do good while doing well."
Joseph Michelli -New York Times #1 bestselling author of books such as Leading the Starbucks Way and The Zappos Experience

"Kudos to Jim Serger on his new book, 2000 Miles on Wisdom. Jim again has told a story based upon his personal experiences and achievements to take what some believe to be a complex issue - customer service and break it down into simple to understand, practical and usable concepts. If you're in business, 2000 Miles on Wisdom is a must read.

Jim Serger has emerged as an excellent story teller with a message for everyone."
Chris Ruisi, "The Coach" -Author, Business Speaker, Leadership Coach and International Radio Show.

"This book is loaded with proven methods and techniques to get and keep customers for life. You learn how to build customer loyalty so high they would never buy from anyone else."
Brian Tracy – Author, How The Best Leaders Lead

"This is a great story; not about bicycles, but about putting people first. Jim Serger tells a true tale about what it means to create a positive and engaging experience for customers. You can learn from his insights."
Mark Sanborn-Author of The Fred Factor and You Don't Need a Title to be a Leader

"Jim Serger's journey is an inspirational story of determination, will, and the power of the human body. Jim's 1,033 mile ride from Carmel, Indiana to Orlando, Florida for charity makes me wish the his alma mater had a cycling team when he was a student. He shows the entire journey from buying his first bike and then proceeding to ride 2,000 miles in 150 days. It is without a doubt that cycling has a very steep cycling curve, but through the help of a local bike shop, anyone can become a cyclist living a healthy and outdoor lifestyle while changing the world in the process."
Paul Dentel-University of Cincinnati Cycling Club President 2012-2014

"Jim's experience shows all of us that we should never underestimate what we can accomplish if we just do it one day and one mile at a time"
Lee Cockerell-Executive Vice President (Retired & Inspired) of Walt Disney World® Resort and author of Creating Magic…10 Common Sense Leadership strategies From a Life at Disney & The Customer Rules…39 Essential Rules for Delivering Sensational Service

"Businesses always win when customers come first. Serger's true story is proof."
Steve Penker -President Penker Properties, LLC.

"Anyone owning or thinking about starting their own business will greatly benefit from this insightful book. Rarely does anyone have a monopoly on a product. That is why excellent customer service, along with product knowledge, is the most vital ingredient a business owner can possess. I recommend the lessons of this book to all."
Marilyn Serger-Interiors by Marilyn- Angie's list, three time super service recipient

"2000 Miles on Wisdom is a collection of true stories about the lost art of customer service and is a must read for anyone who would like to improve their skills in that area. The stories within this book echoed the words of my greatest mentor, my father, when he taught me what I consider the most important rule of customer service. "If you don't take care of your clients, someone else will".
Brad Toft -Restaurant Insurance Specialist, Kinker-Eveleigh Insurance. Cincinnati, OH

"From the smallest businesses to the largest companies in the world, I can't think of any enterprise that won't benefit from the lessons Jim Serger shares about a small bike shop and how they made him a customer and fan for life."
Shep Hyken- customer service expert and New York Times bestselling author

TO BENEFIT

World Bicycle Relief is mobilizing people through the Power of Bicycles. We envision a world where distance is no longer a barrier to education, healthcare and economic opportunity. We provide specially-designed, locally assembled bicycles to entrepreneurs, healthcare workers and students across rural Africa through sustainable work-to-own and study-to-own programs. We also train field mechanics to ensure access to maintenance and spare parts.

20% of my take of the book will be given to this great organization--one who is giving the gift of mobility to those who need it the most; students. Imagine a world without school buses, mass transportation, cars, subways--you would love to have a bike. WBR is making transportation that much healthier, the gift of two wheels.   ~Jim Serger

*www.worldbicyclerelief.org*

# 2000 Miles On Wisdom

# Jim Serger

# 2000 Miles On Wisdom

# Jim Serger

*2000 Miles on Wisdom*
Published by: Red Bike Publishing
Copyright © 2014 by Jim Serger

Published in the United States of America
www.redbikepublishing.com

No part of this publication can be reproduced or transmitted in any form or by any means, electronic, mechanical, photocopying, record¬ing, scanning, or otherwise, except by permission of the publisher. Re¬quests to the publisher for permission should be addressed to Red Bike Publishing at editor@redbikepublishing.com.

Red Bike Publishing also publishes books in electronic format. Some publications appearing in print may not be available in electronic book format.

Library of Congress Control Number: 2014946411
ISBN: 978-1-936800-13-1

# FOREWARD

Being a business owner since 2008, I have seen personally the payoff of exceptional customer service. I have been up close and personal witnessing what transpires when consumers are treated fairly and with honesty and I have been through transactions that have turned into lasting partnerships.

In this book 2000 Miles on Wisdom we see a different perspective than most business books, we see firsthand from the customer's point of view what transpired and how Jim Serger put what he had learned from a business into action.

Customer service is animate and glowing in this novel. It takes you through the initial interface with a small business and a trek of a life time created on teamwork and a friendship from day one. All employees are in the customer service epicenter and in this book we see firsthand how employees and not just the owner of a business deliver fantastic service.

My business is all about delivering what a patron expects, delivering on time and standing on my ethics of people first. This business book will allow you to see why a small business in this case a bicycle shop is so lucrative and is thriving in a very competitive market.

New business is tough to find, sometimes it takes months if not years to capture a new consumer. However, when we are given the opportunity to interface with a perspective client; that is our moment to shine, our time to put our core into motion-Customer service.

I love my customers, love speaking with them, love filling orders and love making them look good. I understand they have other options to choose from when filling their needs. But like this book explains, there are certain keys to grabbing a new client, maintaining cliental and creating customer loyalty.

I know you will enjoy reading this true story as much as I did, for you will feel the passion from a customer standpoint that all businesses seek out to have.

Scott Golden
President and CEO
Make Your Mark, LLC

This book is dedicated to my wife Tarla - for always putting others first.

## ACKNOWLEDGMENTS

    First off, I would like to thank Nebo Ridge for giving me more than I anticipated and for creating a lifelong friendship; you ALL are very extraordinary to me. I would like to thank my editor, Kathy Fuchs, for overseeing and constructing the first draft into a piece of work; I never could have done it without her wisdom and guidance. I also would like to thank Brooke White for cheering me on to write; she was influential in my first book, Go the Distance, and she said now write another book. To all of the customer service authors whose works I have read, thank you for sharing your astuteness, your thoughts on creating a customer experience. Every single one of you has guided me, influenced me and continues to channel millions of readers daily to attain more epic outcomes. To my parents, Jim and Marilyn, thank you for your encouragement, your contributions, and your love. To Jeff Bennett and all at Red Bike Publishing, thank you for allowing me to share this story with you and for your quality work. Finally, to my wife Tarla and little girl, Maggie, thank you both for being supportive, I love you so much.

# CONTENTS

| | |
|---|---|
| Introduction | 19 |
| Chapter 1 "Can I Help You?" | 29 |
| Chapter 2 The Pack Leader | 41 |
| Chapter 3 Vision | 57 |
| Chapter 4 Patience | 65 |
| Chapter 5 Balance | 75 |
| Chapter 6 Commitment | 83 |
| Chapter 7 Equipment | 93 |
| Chapter 8 Knowledge | 103 |
| Chapter 9 Communication | 113 |
| chapter 10 Passion | 121 |
| Chapter 11 Perseverance | 127 |
| Chapter 12 Bond | 135 |
| Chapter 13 Florida, Here I Come | 141 |
| Chapter 14 I'll Be Back | 147 |
| Epilogue | 151 |
| Epilogue 2 The Return | 155 |
| Notes | 157 |

# Recommended Reading

# INTRODUCTION

"When you do a little more, you stand out a lot more." -Ron Kaufman


Who doesn't know how to ride a bike? As all declare, nothing is as simple as riding a bike. The narrative I am going to reveal to you is how to cultivate a customer from the bottom up-from the ground floor to the top floor, from zero miles to two thousand miles. It is a true story about allegiance, perseverance, and teamwork in motion; all because of gifted customer service.

Some 30 years ago, Montgomery Cyclery in Cincinnati, located on Beechmont Avenue, was the site where I purchased my BMX bike and my Mag wheels. Additionally, this is the same site where I obtained my front and rear hand brakes for the bike. I needed them, for behind my house in the woods was the most ultimate, supreme, optimum dirt track, constructed by the Nelson brothers. At every available opportunity, I was there, doing table tops, tricks, hitting the track at full momentum. I treasured the trail and my bicycle-but I cherished going to the bicycle shop as much and gazing at the Diamondbacks, Redlines, Mongooses and all the hardware the shop had in dealing with BMX. I was all in, and the shop was so considerate to me at ten years old, always helping me assemble something up-to-the-minute, or fixing something I had busted-but I had no idea that was customer service.

I currently live one minute and thirty-three seconds from a bicycle shop. Back out of my driveway, go to the first stop sign and turn right, go to the second stop sign and turn right, drive forty-five yards, turn left and another immediate left and there I am, right in front of a bicycle shop. It sits in a strip mall with a tremendous pizza joint down at the opposite end. It also has a terrific animal clinic to which I take my dogs. So I have driven past this shop numerous times-but it was of no concern to me. This is where other people go who have time, and an impressive, expensive bicycle. You know the type of people-the ones with the bike racks, the tall slender-built bodies, the ones we look at during the Olympics, the ones who run by all winter in the snow-the cross trainers.

On any given day in the spring, summer, or fall and with the winter weather we have had over last few years, a whole group of riders would cut through our neighborhood in an elegant, two abreast formation. In groups of 4, 5, and 6. As many as 25 riders in each pack. You know the description-bright colored shirts, tight shorts or pants, sleek looking hardware-the ones you see on the Ironman competition, or the ones on the Tour de France-all looking fierce, as if they were taking on the hills of Colorado, or the New England countryside.

However, I never experienced riding a bicycle like they were. I would just chuckle at them in the car, or on the front porch as they cruised by. I would curse at them for taking up the road, hogging the lanes, slowing traffic down. "The road is for cars, buddy, not for crazy racing or riding enthusiasts," I would exclaim. "This road belongs to vehicles with four wheels, not the two wheels you are riding on", I would be thinking to myself.

Sports have always been a way of life for me, as well as taking on new challenges. Life is not about sitting on the sidelines, life is about participating. I climbed Mt. Fuji back when I was in the Navy. I used to swim 300 meters, no problem; used to bench press 405 pounds, no problem. I could do thirty pull ups and run five miles, no problem-but that was when I was twenty-one years old. Today I am twenty-two years older. Lifting that much weight and gaining that much bulk was many years ago. My body has since gone through two knee surgeries and, let's be honest; my knees hurt when the weather fluctuates hot and cold.

I am an avid reader, and one day I was reading a book about how to be an everyday philanthropist. It was a very insightful book about how to give back to society. It mentioned many aspects that drew my attention-but one touched on giving strength to a charitable cause and raising money by achieving an exercise routine. I had heard of running 200 miles in Central Park to raise money for cancer, walking the Appalachian Trail for cancer awareness, 48 hour read-a-thons for literacy. I sat there and reflected on what I could do. I had no indication -nothing was coming to me at all.

The next day around 6 p.m., I was taking my daughter to get ice cream when, out of nowhere, there they were. The cyclists all gathered behind the bicycle shop getting ready to take off on the evening ride. The same people I yelled at while driving my car were now inspiring me to do something for others, like the book explained. Riding a bicycle, I thought, was a grand proposal. My friend has multiple myeloma cancer-I could ride to raise awareness and raise funds on his behalf and the foundation's-and, while I am at it, I could bring attention to three other issues that have impacted my life as well: suicide, addictions, and literacy. But first, I had to get a bicycle. I still recall to this day I said "I need a TEN SPEED." The next morning on ESPN, Bo Jackson was talking about riding his bicycle across Alabama to raise money for the tornado victims. It was a sign that I took seriously, and I looked at him and saw my physique and thought I can do this as well. But, once again I had to get a bike. I knew zilch about this sport, other than I was not the Tour or Olympic athlete. I needed direction if I was going to make this a reality. Where do I start? Where do I go? Who should I turn to? You guessed it-The Bicycle Shop.

As you are reading this, I would like you to envision a man who is 5'10"-a man who is 246 pounds, who exercises around five hours a week. I had just finished doing the Beach Body video routine called Insanity. It is the forty-five minute workout that you see on Sunday morning infomercials, the one where all the participants look like professional marathoners, cross trainers, fitness nuts, and spinning instructors. I hung in there for two months leading up to the date and I felt encouraged and motivated to start riding a bicycle. So, I felt like I was ready to try something further -just like I did the video segments. I felt great-I pushed my body in very intense workouts, my body changed, I lost weight, I was drinking more water, I was making healthier eating choices. For the first time in many, many years, I could put my hands on the floor and keep my legs straight. I was touching my toes and able to keep my hands there. So, making this decision to ride a bicycle was not out of the question. I had momentum at my back, and I felt very confident about where I stood-plus this is not the first new idea or vision that I had over the last couple of years.

As for anything in life that is fresh, we ponder the notion of just how far we can reach. I gazed, and daydreamed of riding the bicycle twenty-five miles. WOW, that is a ton of miles!! Then I thought fifty miles, maybe a hundred miles-I even thought I could ride 250 miles in a day. I have always been determined to accomplish a goal once I placed it in the memory bank. Like many visions we see and think up, they are just that, a vision or a moving moment that takes us from reality and puts us in Never Never Land for a time. It is so much fun to place ourselves in dream mode for a few minutes and picture ourselves among the great athletes such as Michael Jordan, Mia Hamm, Andrew Luck, Bo Jackson and even Muhammad Ali.

But as in the business world, dreaming and doing are two different things. In order to have a dream come true, one must first lay out the storyboard and have the notion of starting with the end in mind. Goals are fun, and they are attainable-but visions are longer, more drawn out, and more thought and planning goes into a vision. Visions are made up of short goals, medium goals, and long term goals in order to be achieved. It requires teamwork to achieve a vision. It requires sacrifice and educating ourselves on information we need to help guide us. We have to introduce ourselves to others for guidance and answers. New friends will be made, new roads will be taken, and new paths will be explored that we never thought existed.

I had not been on a bicycle for more than fifteen minutes in the last twenty-five years-just to go up and get ice cream with the family. I do not own an expensive bike, nor do I have any experience whatsoever in this sport-but, that is what is exciting: the unknown, the new frontier of life, the new challenges that are ahead and the outcome of a vision of riding a bicycle more than fifteen minutes. But I had to turn to the pros, as I see it. I had to get up to the bicycle shop and get this started. Quit talking and head up there.

My first take at customer service and bicycling came some thirty-three years ago. My neighbor and family friend, Mrs. Ryan, was involved in the Avon business, and since we lived in a massive, thriving community, it was a lucrative endeavor for her. With that, my first dabble with customer service, on time deliveries, hustling to meet customer needs, and the drive to earn some cash was met head on at ten years old. Mrs. Ryan would get the orders, place them in a pleasant, presentable bag, and I would ride my bike over to the customer's house to deliver the order. The following year, I was the yard boy for the Ryans one day a week, between playing baseball and hanging out with friends at the pool. My parents understood that I needed a little job to understand what it means to make money and save money.

One day I was weeding the garden, and I thought I did a first-rate job. A few hours after returning home, the phone rang and Mr. Ryan told my dad that I needed to go back over and finish the job. Now at eleven years old, I thought I nailed it, but seeing my work I realized I could have done a better job at weeding. Those two summers working for the Ryans taught me a great deal about customer service, and I thank them for encouraging me at a young age to go above and beyond just the basics, to give people more than they expect; as Shep Hyken would say, "Be Amazing" at customer service. Those virtues, as well as my parents always striving to teach my brother and me the values of hard work, being polite, self-confidence, and respect for others, would carry me through working at a little convenience store for six years through high school and college, the US Navy after college, and in the ice business for nearly eighteen years after the Navy.

What is it like to be on the receiving end of stupendous customer service? What is it like to be on the receiving end of horrendous customer service? Customer service-those are such fascinating words. They mean the world to so many employees, staff, and management, as well as the consumer and patron looking for first-rate, magnificent, warming, and reassuring interactions.

We have all been to a drive-thru where, over the intercom, we feel as if the member taking our order could care less. Then, as we drive up to exchange money, we see a bright, smiling face who asks us how are we doing, and we drive off feeling pretty good about the transaction. Moments later, we see they did put the pickle on the burger and now all of the warm, fuzzy feelings disappear. Now, we are mad as the dickens and blaming the establishment for horrible customer service, when in reality it was just one person who completed the order incorrectly. But, we blame the whole moment on the whole staff and company. How often does that happen? All the time-we go in feeling great, and we come out feeling disappointed. But we blame the WHOLE establishment and we hold a grudge against them, always remembering the one bad transaction instead of all the other great ones.

One of my friends had three huge water jugs full of loose change that he had been collecting for years, each weighing in at around forty pounds. Pennies, nickels, dimes, quarters, half dollars, and etc. He took the change up to the electric coin counter at the supermarket and realized it was just too much to load into the machine, for the machine kept shutting down. The next day, he phoned his bank and explained what he had, and asked if they could assist. They replied sure, as long as all the money was rolled properly, they would take it all. Do you know how long it would take to roll 120 pounds of change? It was so much that his bank said NO. Not knowing what to do and talking with his friends about his situation, one friend said he should take a crack at the new bank on the corner. Loading up all three containers, he ventured out and upon entering the bank he was welcomed and asked what he needed. In moments, they said sure we can be of assistance. During the hour he spent there, the cashier handed him $1,200 and some change and proceeded to say thank you. There was no fee like the electric machine would have taken-and there were no gimmicks or hoops he had to jump through. The bank is not a national chain, nor do they advertise, as far as I can tell. But when he got home, my friend blasted his experience over the phone, Facebook, and email-and for months by word of mouth.

For the short term moment, my friend was so electrified to witness another person or facility eager to get his task done, and done accurately. He was so taken by the moment that he went home and told his wife and kids about his experience-but it did not stop there. For the next day at work, he told all his co-workers, his aunts and uncles, his neighbors and friends; they then told their friends, and on and on and on it went.

CHANGE-what does that have to do with the paragraph? It is the whole epicenter of the event if you ask me-not only did he take change up there, but the bank that helped him changed their thinking to accommodate new patrons, and existing ones on a small scale. There was no difference between the sizeable bank and the small bank to my friend-they both felt and looked the same, they both had security cameras, vaults, counters, tellers, drive-thru windows, et cetera. But the variation was that the small bank took a gamble and counted all of his money. Now, did the big bank have the same ability? I would like to think so. The same depository he banked at for years told him NO, but the new bank said yes. Why is that? There is no clear cut answer, other than the tiny bank was willing to take the extra step that we often do not see or experience anymore and that is customer service. Did my friend pull all of his money out and take on the small bank as a new home? I don't know, but the payoff that we will never know is how many of his relatives, friends, neighbors et cetera started using that bank.

I read a story of a family that was visiting their son at college for parents' weekend. On Sunday, a big suit and tie event was planned. On Saturday evening, the father laid out his suit and realized the button on his trousers was missing. Now, at home this was no big deal-he knew where to go to get it fixed, but a hundred miles away he had no connections at all. He found a dry cleaner, asked if they could fix the trousers, and was told it would be two days. With great frustration, he drove and found another cleaner-they, as well, told him they did not have time, and it would be two days. So he proceeded to head back, but on the way he saw an upscale men's suit store. He walked in and told his story. There, two gentlemen looked at him and said, "Give us fifteen minutes and we will have you all ready to go." Sure enough, the man got a new matching button put on. When asked how much he owed, they responded with, "No charge." The man was taken by the gesture and pleaded that they take something in exchange-once again they said no, free of charge. I am sure it cost no more than five dollars to fix his pants, but they stopped what they were doing and fixed his missing button. Why? Well, once again, the term vision, which reflected customer service, played a role in this business-as they saw it, five dollars was no big deal, but to the gentleman it was a huge deal. The next day at the event, the father proceeded to tell his story. I am sure he felt a little awkward telling it-broken pants is not a subject we talk about, but he told them everything that happened. The family does not visit the campus too often, but the next time they were there, the father stopped and bought three suits. He later learned from his son that a few other parents stopped and bought suits there as well. Five dollars turned into, let's say, $10,000. Did the owners of the store really think that that would happen? NO. That is just how they run their business; the customer comes first-no questions asked. Once again, the vision of the store owners is what turned this five dollar event into a cash payoff of $10,000. The difference between the cleaners and the store was management and the skills they provide their employees-the difference is change.

The three stories are very similar-we hear them all the time. We get frustrated and a new individual or event happens and we get a huge smile or frown on our face. The simple things are made hard, and the ones we never think would help, come through. Why is it when we visit the hardware store and ask where the hammers are, our first thought is the employee will point and walk the opposite way? We pull into a car lot and are barraged by a staff member, not even allowed to walk the lot for a few minutes, and we have our guard up like a prize fighter trying to keep them in their corner. Then the minute we do need help, there is no one in sight for miles and miles-we find ourselves wandering around aimlessly looking for someone, then we just get in the car and drive off. Customer service is a fun and gifted perfection. It is a perfection that comes with the territory of dealing with people on a daily basis-it is taught, or is it?

I would like to consider that folks have it in them to put others first-then I also like to think individuals are educated to put others first. When an individual is trained to understand that the business interfaces and talks with customers on a day to day basis, this should have been explained in the interview. The initial interview is what sets front runners apart from the back burners. Yes, national chains and small businesses need to recognize that ALL will have to come to the conclusion that everyone will talk with a customer on an hourly basis-some will have easy questions and others will have complicated questions. However, each member must comprehend how to handle the occasion, and how to rise above the rest in giving the answer. All customers figure out when they receive the runaround, aisle four, aisle five, aisle six, and still unable to locate the item. We realize not all have been there five, six, ten or twenty years, but what I still don't understand is why people are so frightened to tell others, "I have no idea, but I will get the correct person to handle you."

The story and the events that I am about to share with you are a true narrative of my experience at a bicycle shop-this is where I learned the true value of customer relationships, the notion of an extraordinary manager, skillful employees, and excellent interaction with clientele. What I have taken from this ride (no pun intended, but perfect fit) is that all stores, shops, salons, restaurants, and supermarkets can see the value of making customer service a top priority. This is not set in stone and I am sure there is more to it than this in other outlets, but this is my take-keep it simple. Keep it on the front burner, and make it a priority. Who knows where your business will be in three years, but maintain what you have and excel at making customer service a priority every single day-for the minute you let your guard down, another business will gobble up your customers.

This book is broken down into fundamental points that I have found to be the most essential to making a great occurrence become an epic experience-one that will last for eternity. One that will draw others, like the baseball field in Iowa, to which I am sure people are still driving. If you build superb customer service, they will come. Trust me, and just like in the movie they will come for no other reason than to enjoy and be comforted. Let's face it-people will pay 10% more knowing they experienced a great transaction. They also will discuss, reveal, and communicate with others about their encounter-and those are advertising dollars well spent.

# CHAPTER 1 "CAN I HELP YOU?"

"I am looking for a ten speed."

"Life is like a ten speed bicycle. Most of us have gears we will never use."-Charles M. Schulz

With everything in life, there is a start when it comes to a new endeavor. There is also a start with every single transaction that occurs in a partnership -the first handshake, the first phone call, cold call, the first email, the first speech, the first presentation. So much anxiety and anticipation is brewing that sometimes we can hardly contain ourselves because of the hype we have built up. I remember the morning that I planned on heading to the bicycle shop to get the ball rolling. It was May 16, 2012, a day just like any other day. It was a Wednesday, and, I had the day off. I got up that morning before my wife and daughter-I made my coffee and grabbed the computer and logged in to the bicycle shop website. I checked to see what time they were opening and it said 11:00 a.m.

My wife got up around 6:00 a.m.; on my day off, I usually sleep in till 6:45 and get up with my daughter. But that day I beat everyone up. I had my coffee made and I had already emptied the dishwasher from the night before. At 6:00 a.m. on the dot, the alarm went off and down the stairs came my wife. As usual, she asked what I was doing up so early, and I replied I could not sleep and we left it at that. But the cat was out of the bag; she knew something was out of the ordinary. At 6:45, I headed up and proceeded to wake up my daughter. I prepared her breakfast, got her clothes out, and offered to drive her to school. Both my wife and daughter looked at me and said, "What is up with you? You are acting all weird. Now, I am a very high-strung guy, and I often pace when I am bored or when I need something to do. That morning I was pacing, back and forth-kitchen to family room, family room to dining room, dining room to foyer. At 7:30, I said to my daughter, "Let's get ready for school", She brushed her teeth and I brushed her hair, gave her allergy medicine, and got her coat on, and out the door to the car we went. I told my wife to have a great day at work and that I love her. She looked at me and asked, "What are you doing today?" I replied, "The usual," which meant cleaning the house; that was my job in the middle of the week-three dogs can get pretty hairy and if you don't stay on top of it, gets out of control.

By 8:00 a.m., I was back in the house. I made another pot of coffee; not that I needed it, but it was just part of my daily routine to make another. I looked at my watch and saw that I had three hours till the doors were open at the bicycle shop. It felt like I was going to a World Series game; so much adrenaline was flowing. I could hardly contain myself. I started cleaning the family room, then the rest of the downstairs, and then I proceeded upstairs and cleaned as if I were still in the Navy. I felt like I had not seen land in thirty days and we were pulling into Thailand for a port call. I was bouncing around, jumping off the walls, as if that was helping. I still remember I had the stereo blaring and I was singing like I was watching The Who concert live. By this time, all levels were cleaned, all bathrooms were scrubbed. All the clothes were put away, the closets were organized, the morning dishes were in the dishwasher and out of the sink, the floors were mopped, and the carpet was vacuumed. I looked at my watch and it was 10:30-I had thirty minutes to get ready.

At 10:55, the launch sequence commenced. Five minutes till go time, as if I were at Cape Canaveral. It really had been a countdown-I was so keyed up. At 10:58, I headed up to the shop and at 11:00 on the dot I was in the lot. About five other vehicles were there, and mine was the only one without a bike rack on top of or on the rear of the car. I sat in my Jeep wondering what they would say. Are they going to laugh at me? Are they going to say we don't serve your kind? Then I laughed at myself for talking myself out of going in. This is what a new concept is all about; it's about taking the first step. It is easy to have a vision, but it is hard to take the first step and this was the piece of the puzzle I had to put into motion. Sure I could have driven to a big retailer, and bought a bike way in the back corner, the place where the cameras monitor you-the place where the alarms go off because you are in the corner and no one can see you. I knew I had chosen the right option; I had to go in. What was I so apprehensive about? It felt like I was asking a girl out on a date, what is the worst she could say-NO. Then we go on with our lives; just like that day, what was the worst they could utter?

I walked in and, sure enough, the place was just overwhelming; there were bicycles all over the place. Shelves filled with helmets, shoes, bells, bottles, nutrition, socks, jerseys, bibs, shorts, gloves, sunglasses, and anything else your bicyclist would call for. For the record, the minute I came in a gentleman was sitting behind the counter assisting another gentleman with his purchases, but he made a point to welcome me. He could have ignored me, but he recognized a customer walking in. I veered off to the right and there, directly in front of my eyes, were the bicycles I had seen all the members sitting on behind the store. I have seen intense colors before, but these were literally a pack of skittles candy exhibited perfectly in front of me. The colors of the bikes were just striking -they were breathtaking. I have always been one for unbelievable equipment, but these were top shelf. Bright greens, whites, reds, blues, and yellows, all lined up at least seventy-five across the bottom and seventy-five across the top rack. The blackest, sleekest looking bikes were displayed and the whitest of white with red and lime green trim were there. My eyes were just so big, and I mean literally. I was taken back by how much serious hardware they had on exhibit.

I glanced over at the gentleman who was still assisting the customer, so I started to look at the prices. There were bikes for $2,500, $3,000, $1,500, $4,000. WOW! I thought I was just looking for a $500 bike. I paced down the display of bikes looking at all the prices and, sure enough, not a single one was below $1,200. I was thinking, "What am I doing here? These are way out of my price range, plus I am just riding for charity, not to invest time and money into a sport eternally." I turned around and, the gentleman was heading right towards me. He extended his hand in welcome, and told me his name was Brian. A warm smile came across his face, and a hearty handshake greeted me. I felt good, and I felt at ease when we shook hands. He proceeded to ask how he could be of service so I told him I was thinking about taking on the sport of cycling. He asked if I'd ever been cycling before, and of course I said no. He asked what kind of bike I was looking for, and I answered with a ten-speed. Now the look on his face was a slight smile, as if full laughter was about to happen , but he looked me dead on, and told me as politely and sincerely as he could that the store did not carry ten-speed bikes, and that term had not been used for years. I mentioned that I had a ten-speed bike thirty years ago, and it was remarkable, to say the least.

I had no idea ten-speed bikes were no longer in use. The gentleman was very eager to enlighten me that the sport of cycling had grown a hundredfold in the last twenty years. He explained that the sport of cycling is no longer just for the Tour de France, nor is it only for Olympic athletes. The science of cycling is an art form, for many people see it as two venues in one. They get their daily exercise and they get to see the lay of the land. They are not cooped up in a building or in their house peddling on a stationary bike. He proceeded to tell me that the science of cycling is just like that of any sport-we have four seasons and during some seasons, such as winter, it is still difficult to get out and about and hit the streets, but for the most part you can cycle 300 days or so out of the year. The man was correct; I could tell right off the bat he was educated and knowledgeable, not only about bicycles but about the sport itself. I could see that he displayed the heart of a true bicyclist and also the philosophical side of the sport. I certainly felt comfortable chatting with him thus far.

He proceeded to ask me what I required in a bike. I answered with a laugh that I had no inkling. He asked what the motive was for coming up there. I told him I had a vision of riding a bicycle a thousand miles to Florida. He looked at me and I looked back at him; he knew I was serious, but he was also serious when he asked how long it had been since

I had ridden a road bike, as he put it. Twenty years, I said. Road bike; now that was a term I had not heard of. He asked when I was planning to go on this ride, and I told him 150 days from today. He looked at me again, and said 150 days! I replied "Yep, 150 days from today." He looked at me, smiling from ear to ear, and said, "We need to find you a bicycle-that will be here faster than you think."

The one detail I recall most about that day is that he did not laugh at me, he laughed with me. When I laughed, he laughed; he knew I was not joking, but at the same time he knew I was in over my head. He never said it was foolish, or that I'd never make it. He just said nicely that 150 days will be here fast, and, in reality, he was correct. He was not short selling me on the concept, nor was he telling me no-but in that head of his I am sure he was thinking this guy is a couple cans short of a six-pack. He needs a lot of support and we can provide him that cooperation. He is going from 0-1000 miles in 150 days, plus he still has to train. Crazy notion, but what happened next is what sets this place apart from other business outlets I have seen or come in contact with, the notion of what is important in business-the business of revealing the truth to the customer.

Let's face it, I was there to purchase a bicycle-I wanted to strut out of there with a piece of equipment. I was on a mission to purchase something that I could take home and hop on and cruise the streets. But, the store representative put me first and himself second. He told me the truth, and that is why this book was written. That is why I had to share with you, the reader, how a business continues to flourish year after year. The truth hurts, but in this situation, being straightforward and brutally honest is how customers are won over. It is what sets the pack leaders out in front, and sets the rest to the rear, or to extinction. I could tell that this man was having a vision of how they could handle my experience, but at the same time he could have ruined the sale for the store. A sale equals dollars, and dollars equal profits, and profits are what keep the doors open. In this case, there was no sale, no profit made-but I had a vision and so did he.

I continued to look at the array of bikes on the racks with him, and he said, "Let's look at them and get an idea of what you will need." We looked at the selection and he told me the names of the bikes-Scott, Ridley, Eddy Merckly, ROKH, Pinarello, Cannondale, Moots and others. He proceeded to tell me that each bike is of a different size, different metal source, and different specifications as to the rider's needs. He explained that I would need a road bike, which consisted of metal, steel, aluminum, carbon or titanium frames. He explained the advantage that each one can absorb the road impact greater than the other-titanium was the best, and steel was the worst. Each bike he had on display, he said, was the best bicycle the store carried based on the reviews, quality, demand, and manufacturer. He explained that the difference between his store and the big retail giant is that these bikes are top-notch, not just mass-produced. He explained that most investments are for the long term and not for the short term. The giant would be great for a short term, but these were designed for the long-term athlete and rider who had a goal of riding all season more than twenty-five miles per week. Based on that information, the bicycles he carried were created to run multiple seasons, or even five to ten years.

He looked at me and said you are a beginner, one with no background whatsoever in this sport. He was correct. He also proceeded to explain that, in my case, a low-end bike would be the best investment. He stated most people need to get adjusted to the new sport-they need to see if they enjoy it. He said 99.9% of all new riders do enjoy it. But that day, one thing stood out. He asked if I would continue to ride after the trip was over. "Probably not," I said, and I laughed. He then laughed as well, knowing that I was being honest with him. We looked at the prices and I just said these are way too high for me-I am a beginner, and I am on a mission. I have to watch my investment to get a good return. He explained that in all new venues we take on the initial cost, and it is going to be expensive. A new house-you have to buy a refrigerator, stove, microwave, garage door opener. Off to college-you have to buy books, pens, paper, and a new computer. He said the initial cost of something new is expensive; little items add up $50 here, $100 there and, of course, $1500 just to get the main hardware.

We went on to converse again, now regarding my physical ability. He asked how much exercise I'd done in the past year or so and I told him I had worked out five hours a week. I told him I have always enjoyed taking on new projects, and learning a new skill-he looked at me and said 150 days from today your mission will be over. He asked if I had any ailments that hurt when I exercise and I told him of my two prior knee surgeries and the residual knee pain; some weeks they will ache every single day. The truth came out; he asked if I was willing to invest fifteen to twenty hours per week training for this mission? Of course, I said yes, I am, and he replied if that was the case, he needed to understand a few things about me. First, are you capable of investing money into the project to get it started? Second, are you going to quit if you find it too hard to keep training? QUIT-I said; I will never quit. He said not mentally quit, but physically have to stop the routine.

QUIT-I have never given up on a goal or a vision in my life and today I was not about to have someone whom I just met, go throwing that word into my vocabulary. But, I looked at him and thought to myself, "What if he is right? What if my body does shut down and I blow my knee out again." What he was stating was the honest truth-he had no clue how severe my knees ached when the weather changed; he also had no indication that I needed to stretch more than I was doing. He was a straight shooter-he was looking out for me, the customer. Why was he looking out for me? Just sell me a bike and move on. Bag up this sale and get back to the pros, I was thinking. But he cared about me and my ability to muster up to this challenge-my vision of the day was different than his vision. He saw me as a newbie, and I saw myself as a road warrior. He saw me as a person and I saw myself as an Olympic athlete. I was on cloud nine dreaming about crossing the finish line, and he was, in reality, just trying to determine what would best fit my needs.

He proceeded to explain the benefit of buying these bikes from his shop-I'd get a free fitting with every purchase and a one-on-one testing on their rack to determine which frame best fit my height. He explained the benefit of the fitting-the seat must be adjusted correctly and, with bad knees, it would be very important to adjust my seat correctly. He also explained that the handlebars must be in the correct place so your hands don't go numb, and your elbows are not locked when riding long distances; the object of the ride is not just to finish, but to be comfortable on the journey. The finish line is wonderful, he stated, but the journey is the best element. Taking in all the new scenery and doing it in comfort is how the game is played.

That all sounded remarkable to me. It was extremely impressive to see the treatment and the attention to detail this gentleman was sharing with me, but all I wanted to do was purchase a bicycle and get home.

I was on cloud nine when I entered the store, but I was taken back to ground level over the last hour I was there. I began second-guessing the notion of the ride, the purchasing of the equipment, the status of my vision. I thought I had good intentions but in reality I was just not fit to take up this ride, and my wallet was not bursting with thousands of dollars to spend at will. He could see that my sizeable smile and energy level were starting to decrease with every word out of his mouth, and he knew I was overwhelmed with all the new terminology and taken aback by the equipment I needed. He was doing his best gig on explaining, but he could sense that I was drifting off from the fun part and headed for a black hole. I could tell he had been in the business for a while. He had been a rider for years based on his knowledge, and I could see that he cared more about me than about any sale he could finalize.

Finally, about an hour into my visit, he asked me what I wanted today. I told him I wanted a bike to get started, but was apprehensive that my knees were going to hurt, troubled about the high cost of a bicycle, and concerned about the start-up price of the other necessary equipment. He said, "Let's be honest. If you don't envision yourself riding a bicycle a year from now, then your best bet is to go to the big retail store and buy a cheap bike and ride with little investment, or find a friend who has a bike and ask him if you can borrow it to try it out. Start off slow a few miles a day and build up to twenty-five miles, and see if you can handle the impact of the ride both on your knees and on your wallet." He was being so honest with me-he could lose this sale, I thought. Why would he want me to go somewhere else? Why is he helping me watch my dollars? He said, "The last thing is, I want you to enjoy this sport-and the best way to do this is to make it as easy as I can for you." As he'd said earlier, his bikes were the best quality for the price, and the store determined that these were the least expensive they would provide for a customer.

I had gone there with the expectation that they'd have two or three bikes to choose from, and one of them would be in my price range; I would grab the cheap bike and off I would go. But right there in that moment of his honesty, they won me over. No matter what decision I was to make-buy from them or a big retailer or get a friend's bike-that store was going to get my business someway, somehow. The man put my needs first and his needs second. Why? Because his vision, his guidance, his gift is what I needed to hear. He could have put me on a bike and said go get 'em-but he didn't. He proceeded to guide me on a few other things-he said to check out the internet, Craigslist, garage sales, or eBay for cheap bikes. He was watching out for me; He confirmed that whatever choice I made, they would still help me. I was more than welcome to bring my bike up there to get fitted correctly, for a fee. They could also check the safety of my bike, for a fee, and guide me in selecting a helmet, jerseys, new chains, brakes, wheels, handlebars, et cetera.

He said, "Jim is there anything else that I can help you with?" And of course, I said no. I was star struck and confused about what I needed to do. He got a card out of his pocket, filled in the store hours and stuck his hand out, and again, with a firm grip, said, "It was very nice to meet you, Jim, and good luck with your decision, we are here anytime." I proceeded to say thanks for the guidance, and the talk-thanks for explaining the benefits of a quality bike. I looked over and, sure enough, there were a few more new customers in the store and I heard him say hello and welcome to them, as well as offer a handshake. It was not only me, but he was doing the same thing over again with another patron. He started his conversation with, "Hi, can I help you?" We introduced ourselves, and finished with him remembering my name. My name is Jim, his name was????? Well, I didn't remember. But he recalled mine-he had a knack for relationships. He had a knack or a gift, I would say, for remembering. Is that taught, or does it just come naturally? I would say it's a natural gift. He meets so many new people each day, that if he can just finish with the name, that will set him apart from the competition-or will it?

I left the store in a black cloud of disappointment because I did not purchase a new bike, but, I had a huge smile on my face and a new outlook on my vision. I felt very confident that I made the right choice in visiting the bicycle shop. I had no idea how much effort one person could put into another until I had the experience with him. He cared enough to throw out many options for me-he was not concerned with the sale of a new bike, he was concerned that I understood what I was getting into. His customer service was above and beyond anything I have ever experienced in my life. Sure, I have had great experiences before, who hasn't? But listening to him, watching him explain the circumstances to me was just unreal. I am sure he wanted a sale that day.

I am certain he would have liked to have locked me in with a huge purchase, but then again, maybe not. His heart and soul were in that shop. His personality mimicked what the store manager had imagined in his vision of opening the store. Treat people right and they will come back- they will come back because we want them to come back. We want to make the right choices for them; the dollar is not the bottom line. A vision is just that, a long-term event. Was I going to go back? I had no idea when I entered the store that morning; but, in the months to come, I was to go back over fifty times. YES, fifty times I would go back!

Why would I go back fifty times? Great question, and the reason is personal interaction. The same reason we go back to the same restaurant, the same barber, the same dealership, the same spot for vacation. We go back because we feel welcomed, we feel at home-we walk in and they know our name. We feel like we are in a segment of Cheers. I used to work at a convenience store when I was 17 to 21 years old. This store was surrounded by a thousand homes, and every single day this place was packed from sunup to sundown. Why? The owners shared what this bicycle shop offered-comfort.

When I got home, I made lunch and sat there and thought about the past hour's interaction at the bicycle shop. A few words came to me to describe what I had experienced, and gradually, more words were coming into play: vision, patience, balance, commitment, bond, knowledge, communication, equipment, passion, and perseverance. All of those words are the backbone to any transaction of this magnitude. However, these words also best describe what all people are searching for in quality. We search and search for the purest of diamonds. We search and search for the rarest of dinosaur fossils. We search and search for the best candidate for president. We continually dig deep into the foundations of the structurally sound to find out what makes them tick.

So many people talk, teach, and share the leadership and vision of Walt Disney. Many books have been written about the legend. One that stands out is How to Be Like Walt by Pat Williams. Why do people care what Walt Disney did and stood for? Why do we share with others his accomplishments? Why do we continually get excited about the new Disney movie? Why is that we drive or fly thousands of miles to visit a place? Why is it that people come to this amusement park from out of the country? Is it the rides, the ice cream, the train, the castle, and the fireworks? We can get those and save a ton of money right here at home. Why is it that every single time I go there I feel like I am king of the world-I am surrounded by people who smile, who say hello, who greet me from first light to nightfall.

The most insignificant person is saying hello to me-the person blowing bubbles on the sidewalk took a moment to dance with my daughter-she was seventy years old and my daughter at five was so thrilled and engaged with this cast member. The bus driver shuttling me from the hotel to the park was greeting everyone with the purest heart and energy level that any employer could ask for. Peter Pan took Wendy to never-never land to see where people have fun and enjoy life. Fun and games are a part of our journey. Walt Disney exemplified that in his theme parks and in his notion of sharing his vision with others. That is the Encore Effect (1), as author Mark Sanborn would put it. It is what keeps us going back to the same show over and over-we want to experience greatness every single time we go there and we are never let down. We demand and we expect the same outcome every single time we go there-and they never fail at Disney. If they do, they fix it.

I was swept off my feet that day at the bicycle shop-it could have been an apple orchard, a boomerang factory, a widget store. It was not the items in the store that got my heart racing and my brain thinking, it was the individual who raised the bar on customer service. He looked at me and saw a person who needed guidance, who needed comfort and who needed to be handled with kid gloves. He saw an investment right in front of his face; he saw a man who did not have a clue as to what he needed, and he stepped up to the plate and delivered a home run. He could have struck out that day. He could have said no, you can't make it a thousand miles in 150 days, there is not enough time, and I would have agreed and he would have lost me forever. I never would have gotten started, nor would I have completed my mission, or written this book. He saw a person whom he could build up-a person whom he could get a positive return on and build a friendship and solid bond with.

Over the next chapters, I will break down customer service and explain how and why it played a pivotal role in completing my mission. Then I will express to you the importance of using it in your daily routine, your daily life, at play, and in your work. Whether you are self-employed, small or large business, the stories I will share will heighten your awareness of how we must continually keep the bar raised on customer service, for what we do affects others daily and weekly. One small step for man, one giant leap for mankind. Those words from 1969 can still be used today. We need small steps to start our giant leap into a new concept.

# CHAPTER 2 THE PACK LEADER

-the owner. It all starts with him.

"Management is about arranging and telling. Leadership is about nurturing and enhancing."-Tom Peters

I am a huge dog lover, as are my wife and my daughter. We have spent many nights watching the spectacular dog trainer, Caesar Milan. Our family has three dogs: a big one, a medium one, and a small one, a German Shepherd, and two mixed breeds. The dogs each have different personalities. The big one, Barney, looks so mean and terrifying, yet he is the one who is the most warming to strangers as they enter the house, and who will sit on my dad's lap. He is the one my neighbors fear the most, yet when they see him with me, they understand how warm and assertive and well-behaved he is.

The medium one, Chewy, is a clingy dog, and she also was our first dog, obtained twelve years ago. She loves to sleep, and is very good around people. She loves to play in the snow, go on walks, and loves when grandma comes over. The last dog, Stumpy, is a very tiny mix-half bulldog, half German Shepherd, we think. She is the one we have to confine to a room when the doorbell rings, the one who barks when a bird flaps its wings a mile away-she hears everything. It is funny to be in our household-most days it is so much fun to be around the dogs, but other days it drives me nuts. Feed the dogs, fill the water bowls, muddy paws, soaking wet, one gets out through the front door. It is very tiring to have three animals in the house, but it is also rewarding. And we also have a guinea pig, Larry, and added Bobbi the bunny.

Each animal has its own personality, its own likes and its own dislikes. Just as in business, my wife and I have to understand that in order for our household to be calm and orderly, we have to be calm-some days it is easy, other days it is hard. But it is my job to ensure the pets are taken care of, as well as my wife and daughter. I would say my wife is the pack leader and she is the one most understanding of the dogs' needs. She knows when to give them baths, when they are bored, when they need exercise, and when they need discipline. The pack leader then shares her information with my daughter and me. My daughter really grasps what my wife is displaying, and she puts what she learns into motion all the time-repeat, repeat, and repeat. My wife is an excellent example of how one should lead-for she also is the owner and the trainer, the teacher and the student. She keeps going and going. We all know a leader can be anyone, but a CRO is what a leader is. Chief Repeating Officer-repeats, repeats, and repeats some more-that is how victories are won, this is how we drive the message home-we repeat and we keep it alive.

The bicycle shop, like so many businesses, has a wide range of employees; there are men and women of all ages and backgrounds working there. To keep balance to the force, the pack leader has to recognize each one's strengths and weaknesses. To quote Caesar Milan, "What distinguishes the true pack leader from the rest? They are honest. They are real. They accept. They are in touch. They are present. They are respectful. They are balanced and they know their pack." The manager of the store has to have all of these qualities and more. Why else would I have left the store feeling so positive instead of feeling so negative on my first visit? The employee that day, on my first visit, exemplified the concept the store owner shares with them day in and day out-take care of your customer and the outcome will be epic.

A few years back, I drove to Ohio Christian University with my father-in-law, Larry Bechtol to hear a great teacher speak. His name is John Maxwell. We drove there that day because I have read a ton of Maxwell's books, and my father-in-law, as well, has read a slew. We went there to hear him speak on a topic that all strive to achieve daily-being a great leader. In his speech that day, he stated that "everything rises and falls on leadership." Rises and falls, rises and falls, rises and falls-I just kept saying that to myself all the way back home. My father-in-law and I talked about the meaning of his statement. We talked about the concept of leadership and how every single person is a leader, whether they like it or not. "People are always watching us," he said.

You, me, the bus driver, the cook, the cashier, the baggage handler, the school teacher, the flight attendant, the passenger next to us on the commuter train. All eyes are on us at all times. If we don't shave, what do people say? If we don't tuck our shirt in, what do people say or think of us? We hear often, who cares what people think of me-I am doing just fine. Each one of us is a leader. It may be on a small scale, medium scale, large scale or worldwide scale, but like Larry explained, each one of us is a leader-we are leading by the minute, by the hour, by the day, week, month, and year. We look at others, we see how they act, we see how they talk, how they dress, how they drive, how they conduct themselves in public and in private. We conduct ourselves daily by choices; some make good and some make bad, but as leaders we have to make choices that benefit everyone, for all eyes are on us.

I attended a seminar for work a few years back. On the first day, we started, as usual, with a lunch to get everyone situated and comfortable and at 1 o'clock the meeting kicked off. As usual, there was the owner who said a few words to open, and then he introduced the man who was going to monitor and oversee the three day event. When his name was called, the man came running up the aisle in jeans, gym shoes, and a white golf shirt. He stood up front and got right to business-he told us the theme of the meeting and proceeded to explain the first exercise. I looked at all the members at my table-each of us was wearing a suit and tie, each of us had shaved, each of us was dressed for the occasion. I looked at him and thought he was not dressed for the seminar. He told us what to do, then handed out markers and paper and we got down to the exercise. He said we had fifteen minutes to come up with a team name, which had to meet the theme of the meeting. Fifteen minutes went by fast, each one doing his best Michelangelo impression, then over the loudspeaker we heard time was up. With that he said all eyes up front-there stood the same man, with the same voice. The only thing was he pulled a superman on us, (no phone booths anymore); he was in a three piece suit, black shoes, with perfect hair. He looked totally different than he did fifteen minutes ago.

He looked around the room and said, "I am now ready to go-I feel the part, I am the part, and I am ready to bring good things to this meeting." He told us that as he came into the meeting, one manager asked him if he had gotten the memo about the dress code. Of course, we all laughed, but he was right. He did not feel the part, nor did he consider himself to be worthy of hosting such a huge event in front of hundreds of managers, salesmen, and the owners. He looked way out of place, as if he did not care and was not motivated; he was simply going through the motions. He knew he was good at what he does, but no one else knew he was. He was not leading through his actions but was simply relying on his excellent reputation. But that day, no one knew who he was-no one knew what he was capable of teaching-and here he was in jeans and a golf shirt to kick off the event.

He did it on purpose-he went on in great detail about the importance of center stage, the importance of dressing for success in order to have a positive impact on others-whether we were a first year manager or a twenty year manager. He said you must want to be the part, the part of you that needs to be all in. He explained there was a time and a place for everything. He was right-for the day I did not shave at work came back to haunt me for a few weeks. Over the next few days, people were not shaving. When I confronted one of them he said, "You didn't shave the other day." Then I confronted another, and he said the same thing. One hour cost me hours of headaches. I am the leader, so everything rose and fell on me that day-it was my fault, for I did not lead by example.

The idea and the concept of a leader is like looking at a tree farm-each tree is of different maturity. Each tree is of a different breed, some small, some tall. Some full and some need filling in. A leader's job is just that, to lead the group to a common theme-but it is also to teach and bring out the strengths of the pack as well. Some need more sunlight, more water, some need less of both. Some may need to be transplanted to another part of the field, and others need to be brought to the front for others to see their full potential. The leader also needs to build confidence in the weak spots each one contains. General Patton used to look at his platoon of forty men and see forty individuals, not a group of men. He saw forty people who were different from one another, different backgrounds, different beliefs, different values-but he molded them into a team, allowing them still to be themselves, but shaping them into a platoon of one. Each one was still funny, serious, quiet, loud, while others had to be brought out of their shells. He formed them into a strong unit-a strong team.

The day I went to the bicycle shop to obtain the new bike was unlike any experience I had ever had. The salesman suggested looking for other avenues to acquire a bike. Now how did he learn this? He was taught this by the shop's owner, who gave him the reins to lead the customer to whatever best fits his or her needs. The pack leader was not there that day; if he was, I did not see him. It was the gentleman who turned out to be the sales manager's job to guide me down the correct path-his job was to coach me into the correct corner that best fit my financial and physical needs. He could have sold me a Moot's titanium fitted bike for $10,000, one that would fit exactly to my specifications. He could have sold me all the accessories that came with the bike as well. But he didn't; he wanted me to have fun, not go bankrupt on my first go-round.

"SUCKER"-the old cartoons used to show an animal (the customer) that would change into a lollipop after he was taken for a serious ride during a transaction. Then they would show the owner of the store with a cigar in his mouth in the back of the store just laughing and laughing about how he got so much money from a character with little knowledge of his purchase. This still happens today; we have no idea what we are doing, so we go to those we think are the pros for guidance and end up buying stuff we don't even need. That day they sold me nothing-zero. He gave me other outlets to find a ride.

The owner of the store, whom I will talk about later, shares with his employees the values of loyalty and honesty. He shares with them his values, which they then put on display with every single customer. The bicycle shop is a small shop compared to a giant retail store; there are eight people with whom I interacted in all 150 days. All eight are led by a gentleman who puts others first and put his needs second. The store won me over, they had me from hello. They saw me as an investment; not as a dollar figure, but a person, and not as a one and done their vision was me returning over and over. They saw me as a walking billboard, not a silent partner. Every single interaction that comes their way does not equal an immediate sale. These are big investments for a person to consider; there are tons of little accessories that add up to thousands of dollars just to get started, not to mention what it takes to maintain a bike.

I was going to ride a bicycle for the first time-I was going to ride my bicycle a thousand miles for charity. I was going to go from nothing to something, but I had to get a bike. The salesman told me to contact a friend and that is what I did the next day. I called a friend of mine and explained what I wanted to do. He replied, "I have an older bike that you can borrow-come by and pick it up, see if it fits, and you can use it."

How does an employee have the right to turn a customer onto different avenues? How does the employee have the right to tell someone they really need to think this through? How does an employee have the guts to tell a customer they don't need an expensive bicycle, they just need a starter? Dollar signs are usually floating in midair when a new customer walks in the door, especially when one wants to go from the ground up in one day. The car lot is a great example-we always think they are going to up charge the sale. We always have our guard up when we hit the lots, but that day I did not. The sales manager put my mind at ease, BECAUSE the owner of the store put his mind at ease.

Vision, patience, balance, commitment, bond, knowledge, communication, equipment, passion and perseverance are ten common themes that every single owner sets on the top shelf. He looks at them day in and day out-each one has to play a role in the daily activities. Each one comes into play every single day, for the owner knows that customer service depends on all of these to fulfill the customers' needs. All TEN must fuse together to make a solid transaction. Something as small as a bike pump means so much to the customer. Do they need the $90 pump or will the $45 one do the trick? Who is doing the buying, the triathlon competitor or the grandma who is purchasing a pump for her grandson?

The pack leader (OWNER) has to educate his employees day in and day out. If it is snowing outside, the store probably is not going to be busy. What vision does he take on? The current forecast is rain and a high of 45 degrees, but come Saturday and Sunday the forecast is sunny with a high of 75 degrees. What changes does he have to make? What accommodations are they going to provide that are different than the current demand? Each moment, the pack leader is challenging himself and his employees to raise the bar higher, to take advantage of the down time to do little things in preparation for the busy weekend ahead.

My first day visiting the shop was a normal day; it was early in the morning and not too busy. But do they handle each customer with kid gloves? I would say yes, they know each customer who comes in the door. Is it a regular? Is it a new face? Each person that walks in can get turned on to a sport that the store loves or they can immediately get turned off and have the door hit them on the way out. Like the TV show Cheers, everyone knows your name. Well, that store knows the names, the faces, the buying habits, and the demeanor of its customers. This is not taught at all. Yes, there is guidance from the pack leader, but this is ironed out in the initial interview. I see people who are passionate about their jobs, who want to be there, who share their passion with the customers because they want them to enjoy the sport and hobby as much as they do. This is the pack leader who molded their thinking caps on a little tighter: the leader has given them manuals, books, and speeches, about making the customer feel comfortable. The employees could be doing that at the retail giant, the big stores, the warehouse type atmosphere, but what keeps them there? The PACK LEADER.

I know that the owner of this store opened the doors to the public years ago to provide a service, not to get rich. If the latter has happened, then that is great and I am happy for him. The owner, the pack leader, had a vision that no one other than himself could see-like Walt Disney had years ago. He saw a tale that has been told over and over again; we have seen businesses come and go, yet this one still remains open. Strip mall stores are vacant all over town, from the downtowns to the suburbs. Yet, his vision is still alive and well. His vision is still the same today as it was on day one. I am sure he has had to alter a few things that he did not foresee, but, unlike many failing businesses, he is excelling because he made a change and he kept up with the times. But one thing that did not change was his loyalty to his customers, his allegiance to them, and his craftsmanship of putting the customer's needs first. I am sure he has taken it on the chin a few times, not even knowing that the customer took advantage of him and his store. However, the positive outweighs the negative every single time. With every transaction the store has done, I would guess, based on my experience that 99.9% of all the customers return again-the 0.1% was never to return. What a great return on investment that is!

Being a business owner is a science, a craft that others just cannot do correctly day in and day out. They have to put a smile on even when they don't feel like it-taxes go up, rent goes up, cost of equipment goes up, mailing rates are hiked up. They have to learn to adapt, to hang in there. Customer service, though, remains the same today as it did in the 1940s-where loyalty to the same store, the same shop, was prevalent. People want grade A customer service; we don't want robots taking care of us. We want to feel warm and fuzzy with each visit. We feel welcomed-and it is the pack leader's job to share that with his employees. Make all feel welcomed. In some stores it is easy, but others complain the minute we walk in-we see it on their faces, the way they stand, the way their shirt is buttoned-we hear it in their voices, see it in their hand movements. We see it in the pace they walk-are they happy? What is their problem? What did I do? Why do I shop here.

When I went to pick up the bicycle from my friend, I wondered what I had gotten myself into. A thousand miles for charity sounds great, but I cannot do it alone. I picked up the bicycle and brought it back home-I looked the bike over and I was so impressed with it. It looked just like the ones the pros use; it had all the components of a racing bike, as far as I could tell. The only problem was the pedals were gone. There were these square boxes of some type on each side of the bike where my feet would normally sit on the pedal-I knew this is where the pedals go-and these square components were screwed in just like pedals-but I could not just put my shoes on them, there were no teeth to prevent my feet from slipping. What are they? I picked up the phone and called my friend. I explained what I had seen and he gave a slight laugh and said they were clip-in pedals and that I would have to get bicycle shoes for those, or go up and get regular pedals to put on.

Now, dollar signs were again running though my head, money, money and more money. I heard a motivational speaker once say in order for dreams to come true, you will hit a toll booth many times. He was right; I had not even ridden one mile and already I was worried about money. The next day, I went up to the bicycle shop and they were happy again to see me. This time a different person said good morning to me, a young man maybe twenty-five years old. He extended his hand and said his name was Chris, and I said, "I am Jim, nice to meet you." I told him I had clip-in pedals on the bike, but I did not have shoes. I explained that I was taking on the new sport and wanted to see if I would enjoy it and if my body can handle it before I say GO. He took me over and showed me the clip-in shoes-Sidi, Shimano, Mavic, Giro, and Pearl Izumi. It was like looking at hieroglyphics; I had no idea which were the best or which ones I needed. He said something I will never forget: "We have ten dollar pedals that we can sell you, and then you can get a feel for the bike and see if you can handle it."

Once again the PACK LEADER, nowhere in sight as far as I could tell, was still present. This kid, this young man, was gleaming with a radiance that just shined beyond his years. Why? The PACK LEADER. Somewhere along the line, the store owner had coached him, taught him, and shared with him his concept of customer service, and the young man ran with it like a script. I was the main character that moment; I was center stage and the producer (the young man) was coaching me in the store values-customer first, the store second. He could have sold me the $65, $95, or $100 dollar shoes-instead he said let's put on $10 ones and try it out. He proceeded to get the pedals and I thanked him. At the counter he asked if I had a way to put the pedals on and I said I had an adjustable wrench.

He looked at me and said that was fine, but I might strip the threads and that could cause damage to the bike and both pedals, the clip-in and these regular ones. He said, I can sell you this pedal wrench, it costs $15 and I said okay. He proceeded to ask if I had any lube at home to apply to the pedals and I said no, I have 10W-40. Once again, he said the lube he carries is intended for the pedals, and it will be easier to put on and take off the pedals. It costs $10 but it would save time and grief down the road-and if you continue on with the sport it will help make the motion of your pedals a lot smoother.

Okay, if you add all of those up, that equals $35. Once again, dollar signs were floating around, but this is a small toll booth. This was the price we must pay to get started and I understood that. But what happened next is the vision the pack leader had of his store. This is the line that sold me again as to their values and their honesty. He asked, "Why don't you bring your bike up and for $25 we can put on the new pedals, take the clip-ins off, and lube and assemble the pedals correctly?" WOW! He was watching out for my wallet and he was watching out for the store. He was looking beyond the moment; he, as well, had a vision. He saw me as a newbie, but he also saw me as a person who really wanted to give this sport a shot. He saw I was putting forth the effort to try and do it myself-but he stepped up to the batter's box and hit a home run-we can help you.

I went home that day, grabbed my bike and my little buddy, Maggie, and by 4:00, we were at the store. She asked if she could wheel the bike in and, of course, I said yes. All of the store associates were busy doing something. The young man was busy working on a new high-end bike and here I was wheeling in what I thought was a high-end bicycle. He looked at me and proceeded to come over; he introduced himself to my daughter and said, "Let's get that bike road worthy for you." He took down the bike he was working on and placed mine in the stand. He looked it over and began speaking bicycle lingo with me. I had no idea what he was saying, and my daughter looked at me as if we just got hit in the head with a baseball bat. He understood and took a step back and spoke to us in simple terms, so both of us understood what he was saying. He explained every single step he was doing, then handed me back the clip-ins and said, "You are all set."

He asked if I had any questions about the bike. I said no, and told him I just needed to get started to see if I enjoy it. He said sounds great-but he finished with, "You got a helmet?" I said no, that I planned to ride around and see if I enjoy it first. He said I must wear a helmet right from day one that my daughter depends on me. He was absolutely correct; I insist that my daughter must wear a helmet when she rides. Once again he was watching out for me, and then he transferred his thoughts to my daughter. Twenty-five years old, and he was tailored to perfection. Who teaches that? The PACK LEADER.

A helmet-I will get my own at the giant sporting goods store on the way home from work tomorrow, I thought to myself. The young man thanked me, and out the door we went. We left feeling good again, feeling like we were put first, feeling like we were seen as people and not as a number. Like I said, the store is small compared to others, but it has a comfortable feeling, a comfortable atmosphere. But it doesn't really; what it has is people who are comfortable with their job and they transfer that comfort to the customer. They are there to help, and I felt it both times I visited the store.

I was so excited all day leading up to 5 p.m.-I knew I needed just one more item and I would be like Greg LeMond on the streets, road worthy. Something as simple as a helmet and I would be riding the pavement, so I cruised on up to the superstore. I headed back to the bicycle section. There were no road bikes at all on display, just mountain bikes, so I knew I was in the right section. Then there they were, all lined up across the shelves: bicycle helmets. The first one I picked up was so cool-dull black glaze, looked like a Navy Seal helmet for parachuting and urban warfare. I picked it up and looked at the size-large, and then on the back it explained it was for skateboarding. Okay, not my helmet. I picked up the next one, yellow and black, very sleek looking, sporty, and it said large, once again not my size. Okay, I looked again, large, small, medium and extra-large-finally a helmet that I could use-I adjusted the straps and tried it on, too small. Not by much, but too small. A sales clerk was walking by so I asked if they had any more, and he proceeded to say that was all they carried. That is it, this is the giant sporting goods store. Now, he did not go to the back room and look, nor did he proceed to ask how he could help. He just looked at me and I looked at him as if to say, "Awkward!" I left the store with a huge let down, but I had a backup plan: the bicycle shop-I know they carry helmets, the young man told me so. Where was the leadership at the superstore?

Once again, I left whom I considered the pros and headed up to the bicycle shop for a helmet. I needed it, I had to get started. I walked in for the third time. They say all things come in threes, good and bad, but so far I was two for two. The third time is a charm, but so were one and two for me. I said good afternoon, only this time it was a young lady standing there with a smile from ear to ear. She was decked out in her bicycling outfit, the jersey and the shorts, and she proceeded to say, "Good afternoon, I am Jama." She shook my hand and asked how she could be of assistance. I told her I needed a helmet, that my head is way too big, and I don't think they would have one. Now to set the tone, my head is so big that in high school I had to order a football helmet from the Cincinnati Bengals. I still have it today, for the athletic director told me upon graduation that if someone comes through and needs that helmet that they would order him one.

    She looked at me with a smile and I started to laugh so hard-I have told that story so many times, and she could not stop laughing. She kind of felt bad for me, then she said, and I will never forget it, "You are in luck, we can take two helmets and fuse them together and presto, you've got yourself a helmet." I thought I was going to die laughing. Here is the thing: this young lady having a conversation with me as if we have known each other for twenty years-this is the stuff my friends would say to me, this is the bits and pieces I would hear all the time from the people who cared about me, and could joke alongside me. She said follow me and right around the corner she took me to the helmets-now there were not as many on display as the giant retail store had-but she reached up and grabbed a helmet and said this will fit you fine. She grabbed the straps and adjusted them; I put it on and it fit.

    Within five minutes, I had a helmet that fit my head-she said they had white or black, and I chose the white. I looked in the mirror and I resembled a mushroom. Dead on, my head looked like a mushroom. I started to laugh, and then she did as well. I said I look ridiculous, she said not as ridiculous as you would be riding without one. She was right. She told me to do a two finger check on the straps, which is how you can tell if the helmet is on too tight. She said the helmet should not come down over your eyebrows, nor should sit back on your head like a baseball cap-this little thing was schooling me in helmet safety. WHY? Because she cared, but why did she care? Because she wanted to be there. Why was she having fun? Because the pack leader knew her strengths, knew her personality, and knew she was a confident person, one who had a personality and one who could bring out the best in every single customer she dealt with. Plus she was being herself, and that is what sells-she was a true saleswoman, and a true bicyclist. She was aware of her surroundings and her atmosphere.

    At the checkout line, we talked back and forth about how I just started the sport, about how I just got a new bike, and how I was all ready to hit the road. Chitchat went back and forth, and she stated that my mission was about ready to commence, except there was one thing missing. She asked, "Do you have gloves?" Gloves, sure I have winter gloves, mittens, and work gloves. But she was talking about bicycling gloves, and she stated that it would be beneficial to use the correct gloves on day one. We walked over to the glove section and she showed me their collection on display. She said her favorite gloves were the Pearl Izumi brand, that there was extra padding in the palm section, and that I could also use the back of the glove to wipe the sweat off my face as I rode. Sold, I told her. She took the pair down and we tried on a few sizes and, of course, they felt amazing. She asked what color bike I had and I said red, so she grabbed the red pair and we proceeded to check out.

Three for three-that is a great batting average. Three times up and the store was a hit. Not because they had everything I needed, but because they made me feel at home, made me feel welcomed. I will talk in a few about all ten categories that made this experience successful and will make your business a success but for now all three interfaces were positive. All were of exceptional value because of the pack leader-the proprietor knows he can't be around all the time. She knows they have a life outside of work, and they entrust their employees to carry out their mission day in and day out-whether they are there or not, the mission is in place.

What if they blew it on the first trip? Well, I would have gone elsewhere. I would have taken my buying to another store, or maybe I would have lost interest in my objective and the dream of riding a thousand miles would have gone astray. Here I am writing a book about a bicycle shop-something we drive by all the time while going to the bank, to the cleaners, to the market; not thinking about what takes place inside that little shop. But it is not only here where quality service is number one; it is the ice cream shop, the yogurt shop, the shoe store, the nail salon. Customer service is number one on radars spinning 360 degrees every single day; they are picking up new clients and are maintaining current customers. The bar who has had the identical beer driver for ten years still expects excellent quality from its driver, and the vendor still expects his driver to give quality service, even though they know each other very well. Nothing slides, nothing gives, and day one is still the same as day five thousand. All of this stems from the pack leader, keeping customer service at the top. Keeping the topic alive and well, keeping the mission statement from getting too dusty. Keeping it clear and readable is the owner's job; hiding it and just bringing it out when it is needed is not the way this store conducted itself. It was on display from the moment I walked in to right now as we speak.

On all three occasions, there were three people who raised the bar on customer service-for they were not selling me the bicycle shop, they were selling me service. Service was present from the first day I made the choice to visit and service was apparent in the second and third visits. Service was a huge commodity in the 50s, 60s, 70s and early 80s. My brother's father-in-law owned a full-service gas station, and today his daughter owns the station. I remember in 1999 I had to get four new tires put on that I purchased, and he said bring it up and we will take care of it. In the half hour I waited to be seen, I watched all the cars come and go. FULL SERVICE–this gentleman was sixty-five years old with two employees and back and forth they went to the gas pumps, pumping gas for all that would pull up. Gas was a little higher here, but they also would check your oil, check tire pressure, check windshield fluid, check wiper blades and make recommendations to the driver. Rain, snow, hail, or sunshine, they were out there providing a service to their guests.

Here it was twenty years later-most full-service gas stations were closed, but this one was still thriving. Sure, it helped that some had come and gone, but what did not change was this man's attitude toward providing a service to his customers. People would drive twenty or thirty minutes out of their way to his gas station. Bill, the owner, always had a remarkable and encouraging attitude toward everything he did. He mastered it over the years, because he was educated on the value of customer service by leaders he had worked for and with over the years. His return on his investment of service were the frequent customers and the new ones he created by word of mouth. Bill was Bill; he was not phony, nor was he seen as superior to his customers and co-workers. Bill, the owner, was also Bill, the gas pumper, oil changer, air filler, windshield wiper changer; he had many hats to wear, but he wore them with honor, and that is what others saw in him and why his co-workers worked hard alongside him. Bill was not above or below his fellow man, he was evenly balanced. One memory I have of Bill was playing softball with him-he was the catcher, calling all the plays and giving teammates pats on the back and cheering everyone on. He was not born with leadership skills, he was taught these at an early age, each day soaking the lessons in like a sponge, and he shared those with everyone he met. He put others first and himself second, an attribute that is all too familiar to those in the service industry. He did it on and off the field, all year round.

Just like the bicycle shop-the owner is the leader. He shares his vision, patience, balance, commitment, bond, knowledge, communication, equipment, passion, and perseverance skills with others. Three for three-if I told you three for three was great, would you be turned on to that store, to that shop, to that park, to that car, to that experience? Absolutely you would. You would have to observe it for yourself, witness it firsthand, and make your judgment call based on your experience. Will you be three for three? Odds are you won't be. Think of it as the best movie in the world; you hear everyone talking about it, they share how wonderful it is, then you go see it and it is a huge letdown. What were they all talking about? It was tolerable, but not the finest ever. In order for one to receive the greatest experience, one must be willing and able to catch sight of more than just the plot of getting a bicycle. One must hear, feel, and be subjected to the full festivities as an experience and not as a movie plot. The animation was awesome, the music was breathtaking, and the outfits were splendid. The stage effects were magnificent, the cast was awe-inspiring, and the visual effects were fantastic. The plot itself we may have heard over and over, but it is the little things that add up to the experience and that is what the producer must do to separate that movie from others with the similar plot.

It is the pack leader's job to bring out these ten themes every single day; it is their job to make all of the employees aware of the themes and the payoff of keeping them in the front. It was three people who won me over-it was not the store itself-it was people, and people sell business. It is people who carry out the mission statements and it is people who deliver the message through their action.

Buying a bicycle is the easiest thing in the world to do-drive up to any store and you can acquire one. Then you can say you possess a bicycle. Cycling is underway for the season. But like any grand movie that we see, it is the little things that we pick up that separate the Oscar worthy ones from the straight to Blu-ray ones. We never knew it was in theaters, we just see it for rent on demand.

In 1997, the movie Titanic was nominated for fourteen awards: Best Picture, Best Director, Best Actress, Best Supporting Actress, Best Original Song, Best Original Dramatic Scene, Best Cinematography, Best Art Director, Best Costume Design, Best Film Editing, Best Visual Effects, Best Sound Editing, Best Sound Mixing and Best Makeup. It won eleven of them. WHY? The little things, so sit back and relax. Get a soda and some popcorn and read about the ten must-haves in every bicycle shop, for you, as well, can turn your business into an Oscar winner as this place was to me.

# CHAPTER 3 VISION

"If you work just for money, you'll never make it, but if you love what you are doing and you always put the customer first, success will be yours."-Ray Krock

A CNN Money article from August 9, 2012 states that the bicycle is the world's most popular form of transit. There were an estimated 133 million bikes produced and sold to retailers last year, says industry analyst, Jay Townley. That's more than double the number of cars manufactured worldwide in 2011, and a 500% increase from 50 years ago. (2)

Vision-In 1839 a man by the name of Kirkpatrick MacMillan made what historians argue was the first bicycle as we know it to be. The Scottish inventor used levers and pedals which allowed the feet to be off the ground. Then in 1885, John Kemp Starley, a British inventor, made what is labeled the first "safety bicycle," with wheels of equal size, a front wheel that you could steer, and a chain to the rear wheel.

We have come a long way in the biking industry, but in reality it is the vision and the push for more bicycle education that has taken on the increased capacity. Bike lanes are going up all around major cities, which then leads to smaller cities doing the same thing. Gas prices are much higher today, and the increased awareness on pollution, i.e. carbon footprint, has taken us to a much needed time where everyone can do their part in helping out the environment. Plus it helps a ton, like the mayor in Indianapolis, a thriving metropolis, who has a vision of bike lanes, bike clubs, and is a part of the action as well as part of the vision.

I am all for the environment-I recycle at home, I do my part in planting a few trees here and there. But one point that really stands out is how much of a push we have as a society for cleaner air. Years ago, riding a bicycle was seen as a hobby. When I was growing up, it was a means to get from a friend's house to the swimming pool, over to the ball field and back home again. The bike was my mode of transportation-then when I was sixteen I got a car and off I went again, and the bicycle was sold or sent to the landfill.

Today, the bicycle is booming-it is talked about all the time. I am forty-two years old and, as I write this, I know that all of my neighbors have a bicycle, their kids have a bicycle, and even the retired couple across the street has a bicycle. We aren't sitting on the sidelines hoping our environment gets cleaner-my eight-year-old lives in a society where the environment is on the front burner all the time. We aren't just hoping it gets cleaner; my daughter actually knows that we must make it cleaner.

In an article written in Going Green Today, it states there are seven ways the bicycle can save the environment:
1. Reduce carbon emissions.
2. Reduce America's dependence on fossil fuels.
3. Decrease the need for more roadways.
4. Reduce landfills.
5. Improve air quality.
6. Reduce cold start emissions.
7. Protect wildlife.

In the same article, it states that if you ride your bicycle to work just one day a week, you will reduce your contribution to $CO_2$ global warming by 20 percent annually. (3)

Bicycling is in huge demand-it is for the athlete, for the child, for the dad, the mom, grandma, and grandpa. It is for the commuter, the weekend warrior, for all ages. Just open Sunday's paper and you will see all the accessories for a bicycle: helmets, gloves, cold weather gear, et cetera.

Vision is the first must-have in any business. It is the road leading from where we are to where we want to be. It is vision that takes us on the journey and it is vision that gets us up and going in the morning. The owner of any business must have this attribute in order to steer the course, the course that he or she has laid out as the means to getting to where they want to go.

Vision is described in the Merriam-Webster Dictionary as something seen in a dream, thought, concept or object formed by the imagination and the act or power of imagination.

The day I went to the bicycle shop I had a vision-I was going to ride my bicycle a thousand miles for charity. I had set my sights on the finish line before the gun even went off. The store had another vision in mind for me. They had to educate, help, and decipher what I needed in order to obtain my goal. Their vision was a lot different than mine. I saw myself covered with graffiti at the finish line and they saw me as an investment.

I went up and looked at the bikes on the first day, but the sales manager told me to get a bike from a friend and see if my knees could handle the impact from cranking. Also, he was aware that money was tight, and that this was for charity. I was not going to ride across the world-I was more of a one and done, I said. But he saw me going the long haul-a future in bicycling. Maybe not riding a thousand miles for charity, but someone who would purchase a new bike down the road that would fit my budget, and who would start a long, enjoyable sport for personal growth and personal gratification.

After I got the new pedals on and my new helmet squared away, I was ready to hit the road. But where do I ride this machine, I thought? So I went out in the neighborhood and measured from the entrance to the rear exit of the neighborhood and it came out to be 2.2 miles round trip. The date was June 19, 2012, and it was like any other day. I was off work-no one around to watch Fred Flintstone hit the road. I was 5'10" and 242 pounds on the first day I hit the pavement. I had a ratty old t-shirt and gym shorts on, not exactly looking like I should be on the cover of a bicycling magazine. But like the salesman said, I had to understand if my knees could handle the rotation of the cranks comfortably without flaring up. I did two laps around, 4.4 miles. I thought I was king of the hill. I can do this, I knew he was right. But I had to keep going.

I kept a daily journal of all my accomplishments on this vision-and day one was in the books, 4.4 miles. It does not seem a great deal, and I know it is not a large amount, but everything must have a start. The journal turned out to be a great comrade during the journey. I would gaze at it and notice my miles growing, and I could catch sight of my start date approaching. I could look back at the days I did not feel like going out-too windy, too cold, too hot, raining, or overcast-or the days I said I can do this.

As day one turned into day two, and day three became day four, I felt a slight pain in my right knee-I felt the pierce right under my knee-cap. I knew it was my jumper's knee coming back and creeping into my festivities. Stretching, now that is a word that is difficult for me, but that day I had to put more emphasis into my routine than ever before. Like I said, I was forty-one years old at the start of this journey, and I was not the young pup I was years ago; stretching had to become very important as my miles grew.

The flight of the imagination can take us very far in life-it gives us goals to achieve, and lays out a blueprint of what tasks must be accomplished in order for our dreams to come true. A vision is just that, a mental photograph, but how does one stick to the vision? That is the hard part-seeing and believing are two different things. I could see my vision clearly, but the steps in between start and finish are where the real journey takes place. I needed to lay out a storyboard-I had to write down the whole process in my journal of where I was and where I was going-I gave myself time to build up to twenty-five miles.

As I said earlier, the bicycle shop said get up to twenty-five miles, see how you feel, see how your body is adjusting, and take it from there. It took me three weeks to build up to twenty-five miles, and yes, I did that in my neighborhood on the 2.2 mile stretch. One thing that stands out is that I got to know my neighbors on the back end of the subdivision. It was fun; a few men would yell out how many times today? Or when are you going to break out of the neighborhood and see the world? I would just laugh; my friends thought I was nuts just going back and forth, back and forth, but I saw my short goals growing and growing. I had a vision that once I could do forty miles, then I would break the perimeter, bust through the wall, and go out and start another adventure.

My vision was right on track and the bicycle shop was correct. They gave me advice to stay close to home and to not venture too far away in case my leg, knee, or another part had a major malfunction; flat tire, pedal broke or even something so simple as a bathroom break. The frame of mind that I was in now was getting myself up to forty miles. Once I achieved that status, I felt I could really set my sights on the charity ride, for the only three people I told about riding a thousand miles were the salesman, my wife, and the friend from whom I borrowed the bike-that is it. I had to build my confidence up, I had to build my strength up, and of course I had to understand more about bicycling. To understand more about the sport, I had to do my research on how to train for such an excursion. I had to set in motion the vision of me breaking away from the neighborhood and being out among the cars, the highways, the streets, stop signs, and pedestrians.

Two more weeks went by and I finally broke the forty mile barrier; of course, I was ready to head out and jump right in with the cars to see how I could handle all the extra distractions that I had not been a part of. My vision was becoming clearer, less cloudy. I could tell my confidence level was growing rapidly, my muscles were getting adjusted, and I could see and feel with each day my knee pain was starting to fade away. My vision of stretching paid off, my vision of going slowly paid off, my vision of starting a new sport was paying off. I could see the picture of me at my final destination becoming more vivid.

Forty miles, "Way to go Idaho," as the pig would say in Toy Story. My frame of mind was starting to have tunnel vision; I was in the zone. I could see I was beginning to put blinders up to all the reasons I could not do this mission. I was, as the bicycle shop told me, beginning to have fun, for that is the part of journey that was taking shape. That is the vision the bicycle shop had for me. Like so many they deal with for the first time, it is hard for them to sell anyone that bicycling is fun. It is hard to sell anyone the big picture, but their vision at the shop got me to where I was-forty miles. I was fifteen miles beyond what they planned out for me. Twenty-five miles was the turning point for them, but forty miles was the turning point for me. Forty miles-way to go Idaho, something so small to the athlete, something so small to a bicyclist and something so small to me today, but at that moment, at that given time in my storyboard it was a mammoth accomplishment-I went from zero miles to forty miles in five weeks.

Like any business that is flourishing today, the storyboard has to be laid out. They have to start planning each moment, day, week, month, and year. They have to look beyond the moment-they can enjoy the current victories they have achieved, but they have got to look ahead to tomorrow. Tomorrow is the day after today-current situations will change, and we have to adjust our sails in order to stay the course. Some will remain the same-they are still selling bicycles-but the supply and the demand will change. New equipment is on the horizon, new helmets, new technology, new state of the art GPS, new seats, seat posts, new lights, and new brands. Zipp, Pearl Izumi, Castelli, De Soto, Garneau, Zoot, and 2XU, just to name a few, are always looking to the future. My sister works for a major clothing company in New York-she has to design clothes one year in advance of the holiday-so next year's Christmas line is due on the current Christmas, next year's Easter line is due during this year's Easter week. She has to be looking at buying trends, colors, designs, threading, color schemes, what sells on the east coast and what sells on the west coast, what sells in the Rockies and what sells in the plains.

Each person is different in the buying game and she has to accommodate those needs and also watch out for the company's needs. She has a vision, but that vision is explained to her by the pack leader and it is based on what the buyer sees fit. Trends come and go, but what remains the same is people need clothes, and people have a choice to make. My sister's company, like the bicycle shop, has a vision of the customer's need. They know the buying habits, they know what works and what doesn't work, they have done the research, they have shared this with their staff and their staff is up to speed on the trends. But the basic component to a successful company is keeping it simple; keeping it basic for the customer is how we win customers over, how we hook them and reel them in for the catch.

The catch is the sell-it is why they keep coming back for more and why they tell their friends they have a quality product. Keeping it simple is how the customer sees it, and the vision of the owner is much the same. He/she must keep it simple through their communication of their vision. The owner's vision is sometimes seen as just that, a sight of something yet to be seen. But as a store operator, one must be able to share the victories with the staff-share how you sold three bikes to a family, how you taught a person how to change a tire, or inflate a tube. It is that simple-we have got to share daily achievements with our staff, because little victories here and there add up.

I felt that the owner of this store, like so many across the United States and the world, shares with his staff the daily victories. He also sees fit to share what is not working and what is working well. He wants to learn, therefore his staff learns; if he did not want to learn, I feel as though this store would have a for rent sign on the front window. His vision is clearly explained and it shows. He understands empowerment-he cannot handle it all, for he has a life. He trusts his staff, he trusts they will carry out his vision to the customers and use that as a beacon of his establishment for the years to come.

One hundred fifty days is a long journey, but it goes by fast, just as day one seems like yesterday to him. His vision is why the store remains open, why customers enjoy being there-they feel welcomed, they feel significant and they feel comfortable being in the store.

While writing this, I came upon this statement that I heard in a conference call-vision is the heart and soul; we see before others using a much wider scope. We see in Technicolor instead of seeing in black and white, and in order for someone to follow a vision, others have to buy into that concept. I was sold on day one, day two, and day three-my batting average proved that concept-the shop had a vision for me, I had a vision for them and together our relationship was built. I was ALL in.

# CHAPTER 4 PATIENCE

"Do what you do so well that they will want to see it again and bring their friends."-Walt Disney

When I went to pick up the bicycle from my friend, he declared that he was very positive in my thousand mile journey for charity. He stated that he felt very confident that I would reach my goal, but he made one thing very, very clear to me. He shared that over the next 150 days it will be the training that will formulate this dream into a reality or make this dream just a fantasy. He said do not waste your time, go out there and train, train, and train some more. When you are tired, go further; when you don't feel like going out, go out anyway. He had begun to understand my passion about this ride, he grasped the notion that I was not joking around, and he knew I was serious about completing this outing.

When he heard that I was riding for charity, my friend jumped at the occasion and said he would like to donate one of his bicycles to the cause, and with that, my first donation was in the books. But this was more valuable than a monetary donation; this was the equipment that I considered necessary to start. It was a ten-year-old Raleigh Road Bike, crab apple red with Mavic wheels and Continental tires. It was the most beautiful piece of equipment I had ever seen for a sport that I had never been a part of. To me, it was like winning the lottery; I felt like a champion that day. I had what I needed to start and I was ready to hit the road.

Patience is attributed basically to those who wait, and we have all heard good things will happen to those who wait. Have you ever been in the checkout line, and you are third in line and all of a sudden another checkout lane opens? So you walk over there, and then see your original line is now only one person, then suddenly the person you were behind is now gone and out the door. Was it really that important to jump out of line? Were you really in that big of a hurry? If you were, you should have come up when it was not so busy.

Patience is so undervalued in the business world-we want instant gratification. It will come at all costs to a company if they have to have it now. A vision is a long road and it will take little steps to make that vision a reality. But for a business to thrive, we have to pursue the waiting game. We put up the open sign every single morning and we look across the parking lot to see who is out there, how many early birds are waiting for the doors to open. Black Friday is a great example of customers who are there just for the sale, just for the moment.

I live close to a Best Buy store. I thoroughly enjoy taking my little girl up there and playing all the new video games, checking out the new electronics, and seeing what new TVs are out and what technology is thriving. The staff is unbelievable; they are very knowledgeable, very outgoing, and willing to help from the moment you walk in. What I really like is that they say hello, then they let you be you. They do not corral you into a corner and herd you off to what they think is the best seller-they let you graze the field and allow you to browse the store. Sure, after a while of staring at the fifty different TVs, they will scoot over and offer some assistance. Other than that, I always feel I could just raise my hand like in school and they would rush over and help. They understand what it feels like to be rushed, they understand what it feels like to be scared away-they get it. I have purchased three TVs from them, a new laptop, many gift cards, and many videos over the years for my little girl and, of course, I have bought a printer, paper, ink cartridges, and all the other accessories from there, as well. I give them my business all year round when I need a team that specializes in electronics. I am not just a black Friday shopper. I feel very confident they will have what I need every single time. I feel great about my transactions, and I feel great about my experience every single time I head up there-they do not push me, they do not up sale me-they allow me to be me, and they are patient and understand my needs are different than others.

One of the big metal rock bands in the 80s and 90s was AC/DC. The lyrics of one of their songs state-"It's a long way to the top if you want to rock and roll." WOW! They get it, they understand it. They understand that in order to get somewhere, you have to be all in from the word go. There are going to be roadblocks, road hazards, and some stumbling, but as the lyrics state, it is going to be a long way to get to the top. How did they get there? They had patience. AC/DC is just like any other business in the world-they have to stick to it through the fog, through gloomy days, and patience will persevere in the end. The payoff is two hundred million albums sold worldwide and counting. (4)

Forty miles and counting on my bicycle thus far. Many days I just did not feel like venturing out-it was cold, it was late at night, I was tired. Just as my friend stated, you have to push yourself to the brink of understanding that great accomplishments do not come overnight. How cool would it have been to say I trained for a week, then I rode a thousand miles and my goal was achieved? I truly believe that the salesman at the bicycle shop was accurate when he said it is the journey that is the most enjoyable. Back and forth I went in the neighborhood, back and forth, pretty boring if you ask any person, kind of like running on a treadmill. You run in one place staring off into the wall or TV, but day after day I could see my miles go up-four miles became ten, ten miles became twenty-five, and twenty-five miles became forty miles. Patience is what got me this far, and I understood I could keep going. I saw my confidence level and my mind drifting off and visualizing me finishing the thousand mile ride.

This early point in the training aspects taught me self-control. I learned and understood the capacity to endure the waiting. This cycle of the journey demonstrated to me that you have got to have GUTS-you have got to have GRIT to endure such a new endeavor. Patience taught me that we have to wait on growth in order to see a positive return. The return, I could tell, was not very close; I could not even see the light at the end of the tunnel. All I could tell was my legs were growing, my calves were growing, my waistline was slimming down, and I was taking shape. But to say I could ride a hundred miles was still off in the distance. Patience got me this far, and patience was going to take me to the next level.

Before I hit the streets, the young man (little Chris, as I would call him later) who put on the new pedals suggested once I felt comfortable, once I knew I was all in the game, that I bring the bike up for a fine tune. They will look over all the components of the bike and see if there is anything they can do to enhance its performance. He stated it would take three days to look it over-so I took his advice and, once I hit the forty mile marker, I took the bike up.

I proceeded in and went to the counter with the bicycle. It was so busy in there that day-people all over the place-so I had to wait a few moments. Eventually, the salesman asked how he could assist, so I showed him the bike and told him I was there to drop it off for a tune-up. He looked at me and, with a smile from ear to ear, stated it would be at least two weeks. Two weeks, two weeks to look the bike over. He said it would be two weeks till they could schedule my bike for a tune-up. Here I was at a bicycle shop asking for a tune- up, and I was told it would be two weeks. Two weeks, now that is patience. Two weeks. Do you know how many bicycles would have to come through in order for mine to be seen? At the time, I had no idea that you had to schedule a tune-up, then again, I was in a sport that I had no idea what was going on-it was all about me and my journey. He knew that I was dumbfounded at his response, but what he told me was the truth. He proceeded to give the bike a quick look over and noted that the tires were low. He asked how frequently I fill the tires up and I responded with not once since I took on riding. Once again, he looked at me with a smile from ear to ear, grabbed the shop pump, and proceeded to show me how to fill the tires. He stated I should fill them at least every other day, and then once I get past fifty miles a day, I should fill them every single time I ride.

Patience is a virtue, I could feel it. You get one shot, no rushing it, take your time and get it done correctly. Here I was a newbie and he took the time to explain to me the benefits of filling up the tires-first, it will allow less contact with the road surface and you can go faster with less effort and second, it will prevent a pinch turn flat, where I make a turn and with the tire low, the wheel would pinch the tire. He stated that the tire pressure is the most important procedure to follow daily, the tire is your best friend. He asked if I had a tire pump and, of course, I did not. He knew I lived close by and he said stop in for air, it's free. He proceeded to ask how my journey was going, and I told him I'd hit the forty mile mark. He asked where I'd been riding and I told him back and forth in the neighborhood. He looked at me and, once again, with a broad grin, suggested that I break out and venture off onto the riding circuit. He told me to take my bike out to my Jeep and he'd schedule the tune-up. When I came back in he had a map of the county I lived in, and he showed me the various routes their bike group takes-seventeen, twenty, twenty-five, and thirty-six mile loops. He said to go out there and see the world, for it is the journey that is the most fun and the benefit of riding a bicycle.

He scheduled the bike tune-up two weeks out and suggested that, in the meantime, I should go out and see the lay of the land, go see it all. He stated riding back and forth is great for building up your strength and bike awareness, but there is a difference between a controlled environment and the roads. He said to carry my cell phone at all times, watch out for cars, pay attention to stop signs, and make sure I carry plenty of water. He said to start off on the seventeen mile loop, get a feel for my new surroundings. He asked if I wear headphones, and when I said yes told me to leave the right one in, and the left one out, so I'd be able to hear cars and people and be more aware of what is going on.

Every single business wants instant gratification, they want the sale now. This bike shop had only sold me a set of pedals, a pair of gloves, and a helmet, but now they have scheduled a bike tune-up for me. Patience is the name of the game-it is how wars are won, it is how the Super Bowl is won and, of course, it is how the Tour de France is won. The waiting game is very unpleasant in business and in life, but the ones who succeed understand that it is part of the journey. Walt Disney had a term called stick-to-it-ivity, meaning never give up, keep going and patience will pay off. Today, Walt Disney has theme parks in California, Florida, Hong Kong, Europe, and Tokyo. Patience got those built, and as I am writing this, Disney on Ice is here in town. Patience built a giant. Patience is what got people on board and patience is what turned Mickey into worldwide icon.

All athletes have heard of the Ironman competition that is prevalent across the world-if you look up the event, you'll find it takes place on every single continent. It is the ultimate test of strength, endurance, and patience in the sporting field-you have to swim 2.2 miles, bike 115 miles, and run 26.2 miles all in a timed event. One business that prospered from this event is Zoot Sports. Zoot Sports was founded in Kona, Hawaii in 1983. Kona is the main site of the premier event in the Ironman competition. A woman by the name of Christal Nylin had a vision of creating a product that would fit the needs of triathletes. She came up with the concept of creating a race suit to cut down on or completely eliminate the need for the athletes' changing area. Through her patience of trying different fabrics, different technology, and different sewing techniques, she designed a product that fits the athlete's needs from head to toe and from start to finish. Her vision of seeing the athlete never changing clothes came to life because of her patience, hard work, and perseverance.

Today, Zoot Sports is distributed across twenty-two countries and even created the first triathlon specific footwear line. (5) Nylin's business is thriving because of her patience, her willingness to play the waiting game. I am sure she would have loved to see her product worldwide back in 1983, but as in any business, the journey is the fun part. Businesses are created to serve a purpose and achieve and excel at connecting with customers. Today, Christal thrives on the benefits of listening to athletes, for, ultimately, the athlete is her customer, and she is going to continue delivering a quality product, which then turns into another sale.

As I wrote that paragraph above, I was thinking about all the needles and thread she must have gone through, how many sewing machines she had to go through. How many fabric colors, fabric styles, and how many pairs of cycling shorts and jerseys she had to buy in order to manufacture the ultimate triathlete sporting goods apparel. Many nights, days, weeks and years she sat there conjuring up the specs on her vision, many flaws, many setbacks, many hopes and dreams she set for herself. Patience is the word that so many businesses that prosper have to give thanks to. Zoot Sports, like McDonalds, was created on the west coast and today both are available worldwide. Now, that is confidence in motion and that is the payoff of patience.

The art of opening a business and keeping it open is just that, an art. The National Bicycle Dealers Association has a great article written about the business end of wanting to launch a bicycle shop. They break it down into the good news and the bad news of opening a shop. First the bad news: they state that 70 percent of all start up bicycle shops will be out of business within the first three years. In the midst of that scare, they go on to share some strong data on the trends of bicycle shops. The number of independent bicycle shops was around eight thousand in the 1980s and in 2004 it was down to five thousand or so. In the report, the association states that a thousand shops close yearly, but a thousand open up to counterbalance the won/lost ratio. (6) Today, the numbers still decrease, which is due to many reasons-I know one as I write this, high taxes, but that is for another book.

The good news for opening a bicycle shop is that there are forty-five million adult cyclists today, as the association writes. They state this could increase with the times-the heightened awareness of sharing the roads with bicyclists would be one reason for a great and prosperous future. The article continues that a bicycle affects people's lives in a very positive way, and it contributes to the betterment of the environment.

Of course, the negative outweighs the positive when opening a business like this. The association is not here to tell you NO, you can't open one up, but they do set the tone for not only this type of structure but also any other start-up business. They are there to share the facts. Fact-it is not easy. Fact-70 percent will fail. Fact-a thousand or more close yearly. Fact-mail order, chains, and mass merchants have the current momentum. This site describes the heartache that so many people don't envision and that is simply the truth. The truth hurts; it is very hard to cope with and understand that it takes commitment beyond today and tomorrow to maintain and prosper in the field of owning a business.

This association's article hits the nail on the head when explaining the long journey of being a store owner. The bicycle shop is no different from businesses such as the nail salon, the barber shop, pizza shop, the local burger joint, or the local ice cream parlor. They all are in the business of selling something. But first and foremost, as stated in this article, it will take mechanical inclination and a strong constitution, including handling long hours, hard work and setbacks.

Patience is why this bicycle shop next to my house has lasted for so long. Patience is what they provide and understand in their commitment to the customers' needs. Bikes fly off the shelves-$1,400 bikes, $5,000 bikes, even $10,000 bikes-and of course the associated accessories. This place is always crowded, but in the past, patience had to take its course. It was patience that the store owner provided his staff, its patience the staff provided their customers and its patience the customers understand in the buying circuit.

My bicycle ride is just that: patience, the waiting game. I am going from zero to one thousand miles. I am not slim and fit; I look like a fire hydrant on a bicycle. But as the story goes on, I will take shape into a slimmer fire hydrant on a bicycle. But, I have to wait and wait, and wait some more, each day building up my knowledge of the sport, building up my daily regimen, and building on the bicycle shop's advice on how to stay the course and what I need to complete my journey. Two weeks till I get my bicycle in for a tune-up, now that is patience. I know the first day the shop opened, there was not a wait to get a tune-up, but today there is. The shop had a vision; they knew people would come. They knew word of mouth would spread. They knew they could provide excellent service, but they had to wait. I am sure it was not very long, but they had to be patient. "If you build it, he will come" is my favorite line in the movie Field of Dreams. It is so true: if a person truly believes what he is doing is right, if she truly believes she can make a stand, if they truly believe they have the determination to create a magical shop, then go for it and the customers will flock there-but patience will make or break you. You must wait it out, do not fold early. As the saying goes, only the strong will survive. Well, in reality it is those who understand and commit themselves to delivering a quality product and service that will win over the hearts and minds of the customers.

While doing a little research on the topics of patience and bicycling, I was very interested to ascertain the location of the world's oldest bicycle shop. After searching for all of thirty seconds the mission was over: Pearson's Cycles holds the official title (7) and was recognized in the Guinness Book of World Records in June, 2012. This shop dates back to 1860, and, to this day, has been in the same location holding onto the same name with a firm grip. The shop is located in London, and is run by Guy and William Pearson, and is now into its fifth generation with the family name. London, England-fifth generation-WOW!!! Now that is patience in motion. Two world wars have come and gone. Now, can you imagine what it was like to hang on during those wars and still continue to thrive today? The horror of being bombed, the horror of being taken over by hostile forces, and the horror of not knowing what lie ahead. But patience is what enabled them to achieve this status, patience is why the store is still open, and patience is why people continue to buy from them, leading to the opening of another store in London. This store had a vision years ago, and has since been through the production process of the penny farthing, the moped and motorcycle generations and, of course, has seen and withstood the test of time with the mountain bike boom. In the 1980s, the store received a Raleigh Five Star status. (londonandpartners.com) a quote by William Pearson really explains it all-"We love the cycle business and thank all of our loyal customers, staff, and friends past and present, who have supported us to reach this landmark award."

Awards are not handed out just to be handed out. Smith Barney said, "You have to earn it." I could not agree more, but how does one earn it? Patience. We don't wake up one morning and say, I think I will open a bicycle shop, and in 150 years have it still thriving. We wake up and have a vision, but we have to put that vision in motion-then we have to have patience to get us to where we want to be. Apple stock was valued at $2.00 a share back in 1985; today, as I write this, it is valued at $125 a share. Steve Jobs had a vision of where he wanted to take the company, but his vision far exceeded shareholders' dreams. The Pearson cycle shop is no different than the restaurant, the hotel, or the new bank that just opened its door. Time will tell who understands it, and time will tell who was just in it for the cash.

This bicycle shop in London is just like the bicycle shop in California, New Mexico, Idaho, Louisiana and Ohio. They all have one thing in common-they sell bicycles-but what separates the great ones from the average ones is customer service. In the quote above from William Pearson, he states that he gives thanks to his staff and his loyal customers. Loyalty-what a superb word to describe his store's journey. It is of the highest honor to have loyal customers-it is what keeps the doors revolving, what keeps the vision alive and thriving, and it is the simplest way to advertise. Loyalty is how the game of business is won, it's how we get to the top of the food chain. We are surrounded by competition all over the place-dentists, banks, liquor stores, gas stations and, of course, bicycle shops. Top grade "A" customer service is what keeps customers loyal; it's what separates the fly-by-night from the structurally sound.

# CHAPTER 5 BALANCE

"Life is like riding a bicycle. To keep your balance you must keep moving."-Albert Einstein

Some years ago, I was in Cincinnati for a managers meeting, and the guest speaker was Gary Jerow. Gary has some serious energy, he is one that can light up the room without even talking and his presence alone can bring new oomph to anyone's table. Gary is the owner of Modern Ice, which is a company that brings years of skill into the packaged ice industry worldwide. Gary understands vision and patience, and his company is nearly thirty years old. Gary gets it. While I was sitting there listening to Gary talk about a broad base of topics, I saw that he brought in his little girl. She must have been ten years old or so-she sat off to the left of him just gleaming in admiration of her dad. He recognized her at various times during his speech, but one moment that I have never forgotten was when he brought a chair out and placed it next to him and proceeded to ask his little girl to stand on it. With that, she stood one inch taller than he did, and Gary then proceeded to talk about balance. He raised her up to equal his build and that, in turn, built her up. I thought it was great; here is a man who comprehends that work is significant, and who has flown all over the country and worldwide, for that matter. Here is a man in a suit and tie talking about balance-heart-to-heart about creating an equal-chatting about how to raise people up to make them feel a part of the team. Gary gets it, Gary recognizes it.

I thank Gary Jerow for spreading his values, for broadcasting his intellect with me and with the other members at the meeting. I have never forgotten his message. The bicycle shop has the same symmetry as Gary shared. The store owner has got to familiarize himself with his staff day in and day out as well as have his staff align themselves with the customers' needs each day. Days change, seasons change, but customer service remains the same. There is a balance that a store owner has to maintain in order for the store to flow-staff will need days off, staff will get sick, staff will be late due to weather conditions. Customers will ask for the weirdest items, customers will make promises, customers will lead you on and never come back, customers will get the information they need and buy online or from direct warehouses, and customers will buy once and never again be seen in the establishment. Most customers will be there for life; that is the balancing act.

Owning a store is the American dream. It is what we were taught as kids-go out and make a difference in this world. Do something for others and they, in turn, will help you feel fulfilled. The owner of this bicycle shop is no different than the owner of Intown Bicycles in Atlanta, Georgia. Here is a review I found on Intown Bicycles.

Mike Goodman has been selling bikes for nearly 30 years and his approach is as simple as it is timeless; offer excellent service, welcome first-time cyclists, and mix in generous helpings of southern hospitality. (8)

This shop has to understand balance, has to understand harmonizing, and of course has to understand what it means to stabilize. Many shops in the United States, as I stated earlier, are in it for the long haul, but others fold without being in the game very long. Dreams continue to flourish in the United States, and bicycles are the talk of the town; mash those two together and you have one excellent start for an excellent future.

Another bicycle shop that understands balance is Kopp's Cycle, which is located in Princeton, New Jersey. According to my study, they are the oldest bicycle shop in the United States, dating back to 1891, which was, at that time, operated by E.C. Kopp. Today, Charles Kuhn owns the store, which his father purchased in the late 1940s. According to Charles, his father and Dick Swann pioneered the import of Italian racing bicycles and parts in 1960 and launched Kopp's to be the hub of eastern U.S. bicycle racing until the late 1970s. Over the years, many famous cyclists, actors, and educators have walked through those doors-from Albert Einstein to Brooke Shields, and of course, Greg LeMond. One piece that really stands out in reading about the store is a quote from Charles Kuhn: "I am very proud of the store's history and I am trying to keep the standards set by my father and Mr. Kopp." The store keeps a strong balance of equipment needed for today's market-from bicycles for two or more, and bicycles for transportation, training, and for racing-Charles states, "We are committed to helping everyone enjoy all aspects of cycling." (9)

Talk about balance-that store is over 100 years old and they have seen it all. The dot-com era, the fax machine, the cordless phone, the iPhone, the Internet, the mountain bike era, the carbon wheels, the BMX age, they probably even had a pay phone out front at one time or another-but that is long gone, I am sure. Balance is what has kept this store thriving, balance is what has kept customers coming and going. Calibrating a bicycle is what operates the shop-but in reality, calibrating is why this store has been open for so long. The winds change, buying habits change, technology changes, however, calibrating the winds, and adjusting the sails, and sticking to the core is what has allowed this shop to flourish. Princeton, New Jersey-I have never been there. But I can imagine what the shop was like before everyone had cars-before everyone had a more efficient means of transportation. Then again today, as we have touched on already, the environment is calling out for help; and Kopp's is right there in the mix, balancing the weight of what they need to carry and what they don't need to carry. Demands come and go, but customer service is why they are still sharp.

It had been two weeks and my appointment was all lined up, so on my last day before dropping my bike off, I got in one last loop around the neighborhood. I did not listen to the shop's advice to go out and venture off-the bicycle was not shifting correctly, nor were the tires riding very smoothly as they were a few weeks back. I was a little uncertain to hit the roads. But I did get in fifty miles, or twenty laps, as my wife would say-back and forth I went. I was feeling really good that day, my head was up high and my step was a little faster than normal. I knew my bicycle was going into good hands, like a patient going in for surgery. I felt confident that the bicycle was going to change for the better; I was depending on the shop to work its magic.

I got home from work, and asked Maggie if she wanted to go to the bicycle shop. With a huge outburst she said, "YES!" We loaded the bike up and were there in one minute. She, of course, loved rolling the bicycle in the front door and it gave her a sense of being a part of the mission. The moment we walked in, the young lady I talked about earlier came right up to us and said hello. She and my daughter hit it off, and we felt like we had been there for years. We proceeded to the back of the store where all the heavy equipment was-the mechanics bay. There were two stands and three mechanics at the time-one was the young man I talked about earlier, but now there were two others that I had never seen. One was a big boy, ponytail and scruffy looking, and the other had a beard and looked like he could just blow you away with his bicycle knowledge. She grabbed the bike and logged the type and age of the bicycle into her computer, took a few notes and asked if there were any problems. Of course, I explained it was not shifting correctly, and that the wheel felt a little unstable. She proceeded to explain it would take a few days to look the bike over; they would check every single component on the bike and call if there were any major problems.

My daughter and I said thanks and we walked around the store. We walked over to the other side where the kids' bikes were and the bikes we see them riding in Martha's Vineyard. There they were, the bicycle horns, and of course my daughter's eyes grew bigger and bigger. She squeezed one and sure enough it gave out a big HONK, then she did it again-HONK-and again-HONK. By this time, the young lady emerged from around the corner to survey what all the commotion was and she began to laugh, for now I was doing, as well. She then came over and did the same thing-HONK. Balancing is an act for which we have to weigh the good and the bad, work from play, and in that very moment she was having a PLAY moment, which showed a side of her that we don't see very often in business. She was a human being; she was balancing the job like so many businesses wish they could teach their staff.

I don't think anyone can teach that moment at all; we either have it in us, or we don't. Businesses are always searching and searching for a way to connect with the customer, and this little moment meant more to me that anything else they could offer. She was happy and content with her emotions, and that little piece of sunshine that day is what sold me on the store's core values and core strengths. She was being herself, a person with a personality and not a robot out walking around aimlessly. She had it in her to say stop that please, but she also had the notion it would not last long and to enjoy the moment and that is what she chose to do. My daughter laughed so hard all the way home-she began to see the shop as a place of comfort and so did I.

At the circus, we are taken aback at the sheer strength of the balancing act. We see the clowns do it, we see the elephants do it and we ask how do they do that? The same questions come up in business-how can they balance all of that? The answer is in the question, if you ask me. Balancing one's life is like a school teacher setting what is important and what is not important to tackle for the minute, the hour, the day, the week and for the month and year. It is a balancing act; many, many items will be thrown your way, and it is up to you to sort them out by priority. As a manager, leader, or teacher, we have a choice of three things: we can run with the ball, we can pass the ball, or we can fumble the ball. Being a quarterback is the center of attention, just as we see the employee of the store helping the customer. They are the center of attention right there, in that moment. They can pass the buck, muffle the sale or run with it. The initial transaction can be WON or LOST in a matter of minutes.

In that split second when the woman honked the horn, she was balancing her life. She was having fun and, at the same time, displaying the company's persona firsthand. Would she have done that with all the customers? I would like to say yes, she gets it, she grasps the concept and she never glances back over her shoulder to see if the boss is watching-he gives her free reign and allows her personality to sparkle, which, in turn, makes the store shine. All of the employees that I had interacted with presented themselves in a manner of I adore my job, and my job loves me. Love is a crazy word, it can go in many directions, but in this case, the store's case, there is an aura of affection for wanting to be there, and wanting to be a part of something extraordinary.

Balancing the vision of my journey on a thousand mile trek is something I thought I could just jump right in and begin my ride. Well, it was supposed to be that straightforward, I thought. The act of preparing for the day's ride for the first couple of weeks was just that, a ride. I did not balance my life very well; I was so focused on getting on the bike that I lost track of what was important-time. Time will tell, we have heard that, but time also requires a vision, patience and a balancing act. It is hard to ride a bike, go to work, eat as a family, read books, do homework with my daughter, stretch, learn about bicycles, learn the bike lingo, et cetera. .It is hard, but I had to become skilled at balancing my days and my weeks far in advance. I had to give myself a little space between what was critical and what was not vital. I learned a great deal about focus and determination in this journey, but I learned more about balancing my day through organizing it. I saw that act every single time I walked into the bicycle shop. I saw them balancing between cleaning the store, preparing new equipment, fitting new customers, repairing bicycles, assembling bicycles, talking with customers. They were very organized from the outside looking in; being organized is how we bring balance to our day, it gives us structure and accountability for our daily routine.

I got off work and, once again, Maggie and I headed up to the shop to pick up the bike. We walked in and there at the counter was a tall, slim man, mid-forties. I had never seen him before. He wore glasses and with a soft voice, he extended a warm welcome to my daughter and me. He said his name was Tim and asked if he could help and I said we were there to pick up my bike after a tune-up. He ushered us back to the mechanics bay and there, on the rack, was my bike. The young man proceeded to say it would be one more day. My daughter looked disappointed with this news, so we ventured off and looked around. The tall man noticed she was a little down, and he asked her, "Can you catch?" She said yes and, with that, he threw her a company logoed water bottle. She caught it and her eyes grew as big as a cantaloupe. Now he did not throw me one, for the record; he threw the little eight-year-old a piece of plastic not worth more than five dollars, but to her it was a million bucks and to me it was a very nice gesture. He could have done nothing, but he balanced a negative with a positive. A positive moment was created again here at this shop. Each time a positive was happening-

why???Because this is how the store operates, this is how it functions, this is why there is an open sign on the front door instead of a for sale sign. This is what keeps people opening the doors, this is why it is always crowded on Saturday and Sunday, and in the summer almost all seven days, packed and packed full of people wanting to experience the same thing I am. They can perform tricks at this shop, but in reality they are people who understand balancing is part of customer service.

# CHAPTER 6 COMMITMENT

"If we keep doing what we're doing, we're going to keep getting what we are getting."-Stephen Covey

Any business has to have commitment to establish its stronghold and enable itself to prosper and continue skyrocketing for the years to come. Commitment comes in various forms. First, it comes from the vision of the owner or business tycoon. Second, it comes from the owner taking all in under his/her umbrella and sharing his/her core values with all involved. Third, commitment comes from the customer, as well. The establishment's commitment to its customers helps the customers build a relationship with the business. It is a beautiful cycle once you understand the form it takes.

Owner to staff-staff to customer-customer to business.
REPEAT, REPEAT, REPEAT.

It is that simple. Break that chain and say good-bye to your customers, keep it tight and keep it alive and visible, then say hello to growth. I have bought enough $15 popcorn from the Boy Scouts of America to feed the 7th fleet in Japan. I adore the virtue of commitment the Boy

Scouts have carried on since being founded in 1910. The commitment the Boy Scouts have is 113 years old as of the writing of this book. That is 113 years of solid devotion to young men's lives; the pledge of making something better, something more complete and keeping that vision alive and well is the goal. One item that really stands out in the Boy Scouts is the merit badges. The merit badges are just that: badges that the scouts and eagle scouts earn over the years, and like the Marine Corps, they are not just given. One badge, in particular, that I am going to talk about is one of the original fifty-seven badges issued by the Boy Scouts-that badge is the Cycling merit badge. (10) It was created in 1911, and is required in order to be an Eagle Scout. Eagle Scout is the highest rank one can be in the Boy Scouts-it takes many years of wisdom, leadership, experience, and, of course, allegiance to achieve the status of Eagle Scout.

I felt this badge was a great way to start this chapter-it is an excellent source of information to display to you, the reader, that commitment in the Boys Scouts is the same as commitment in your workplace, at home, at play, and at church. The bicycle shop has the same concept- we don't just roll over out of bed and say today I know I will sell five helmets, four pumps, and ten bicycle jerseys, then walk into work and wish for that moment to arise. They have got to earn it, they have got to display dependability each and every day; It is a test each moment at work, like the Boy Scouts fifty-seven merit badges. The shop, as well, has fifty-seven badges it must display at any moment-it could be as simple as a question on bicycle wheels, or as complicated as a fitting for a new Scott Plasma 30.

The Cycling merit badge does not specify the type of cycle that is used.

Scouts have earned this using traditional bicycles, specially adapted bicycles, hand cycles, tricycles and quadracycles. The requirements for earning this badge are as follows:

1. Display your knowledge of first aid for illnesses or injuries that occur while riding, including hypothermia, heat reactions, frostbite, dehydration, blisters, snakebites, and hyperventilation.

2. Clean and adjust a bicycle. Prepare a bicycle for inspection using safety checklist.

3. Show your bicycle to counselor for inspection and point out ad-

justments or repairs you made. Show points that need oil, show points to check regularly, and show how to adjust seat, brakes and steering tube.

4. Show how to brake with foot brakes and with hand brakes.

5. Show how to repair a flat.

6. Take a road test and demonstrate the following: mounting, execute right turn, execute left turn, cross railroad tracks, proper curbside and road-edge riding.

7. Describe the state laws for bicycles, and know bicycle safety guidelines.

8. Must take two rides of ten miles, two rides of fifteen miles and two rides of twenty-five miles-and report routes taken and interesting things seen along the way. (I love that one-for it is the journey.)

9. After fulfilling the first eight steps, lay out on a road map a fifty mile trip. Stay away from highways and complete this ride in eight hours.(Meritbadge.org)

To earn one badge, a Boy Scout has to go through that course. I will say it again: to earn one badge, a Boy Scout has to go through that course. That is just one item to complete. Now imagine what else he has to go through in order to be an Eagle Scout. Here is the list of the rest: First Aid; Citizenship in Community, in the Nation and in the World; Communication; Personal Fitness; LifeSaving; Environmental Science; Personal Management; Camping, Cooking, and Family Life.

It sounds to me that, in order to run a business, one must go through an Eagle Scout course, and it is so true. The Scouts understand what fortitude means; they comprehend they just can't hand out the awards, which would be defeating the purpose of the journey.

The bicycle shop is the same way-they understand they have got to provide all means of the bicycling world under one roof, everything from general knowledge, to in depth conversations. They have got to do research, they have got to do hands-on training, and they have to be able to handle all types of customers-from the triathlete, to the weekend rider, to the racer, to the mountain biker and to the little tot just learning to ride.

The next day, of course, I was really looking forward to getting the bicycle back. The Raleigh never looked so first class, nor felt so good as when I saw her at the shop. The crabapple red was so red, I needed shades just to grab her and load her up. The relationship that I now was having with the bicycle was starting to take shape-I could tell she had been through a thorough cleaning and inspection, and the bicycle just looked incredible. She had been in the care of some extremely talented individuals, and I started to wheel her out to the Jeep. As I proceeded, the salesman suggested I get another water bottle because of the heat. Two bottles would be a great idea for a big guy like me in need of a little more hydration. Just then, in that moment he was committed to me, and I agreed; the shine of the store took place. A $10 dollar bottle holder and $5 water bottle would prevent me from becoming dehydrated. They installed the items, I thanked them, and out the door I went. Now, I could not see the front of the bike, but I believe that day the bicycle had a smile from handlebar to handlebar when I loaded it up, just like I did.

I came back in and paid the staff $150 for the tune-up, the look over, and the wash up. While paying the bill, the young man told me he had replaced a spoke in the wheel, adjusted the brakes, worked on the shifting, filled up the tires again, and greased and oiled the correct parts. He told me that it was time for me to hit the road running and asked how many miles I had logged so far, and I replied, "216." Now, how did I know that? Earlier, I mentioned the logbook I carried; every single day, I would take notes about the day's ride, and I added up the total miles. I was committed to this venture, and I had to keep track to see where I have been and where I was going. He said that was great for a new rider and to keep at it, the fun part is the journey. And I will never forget what he said next: "Why, all of a sudden, are you riding a bicycle?" Little Chris, a highly educated, college baseball player with a master's degree, was onto me. He knew I was on a mission, but I had to see if I could keep at it before I told anyone. I was confident, but my body may have other ideas, so I just told him it was something new in my book of sports.

Looking at my logbook as I write these words, I saw my commitment paying off. In my first thirty days of training I had ridden fifteen times, so I would say I was committed. But one thing that got me motivated, as well, was the bicycle shop. Every time I went in there, the young lady asked how my start-up was going, the young man asked how my foray into a new sport was going, and the man I saw on day one asked how my ride was going. They all were aware that I was new to the sport. But they always asked how it was going, how my knee felt, if there were any problems with the bike-they always asked. That is commitment to a store or business. The faces are easy to remember, but this shop called me "Jim"-this is commitment in motion. The faces are easy to remember, the names are hard; all the customer has to do is remember one name, but the store or bank has to give a little more elegant touch, and try to remember the names.

I knew upon leaving the store that I was ready to venture out into the real bicycle scene. I was all in-I was still wearing gym shorts and a t-shirt. My butt really hurt during those first thirty days, my elbows were killing me, and my knees were aching. My stretching was really taking hold, my muscles were developing, and my calves were turning into mountains. I could see my commitment to the sport paying off each day, and each week I grew stronger and stronger. They were right at the bicycle shop: go slow and good things will happen. My allegiance to the shop was growing stronger and stronger. My devotion to the sport was growing stronger and stronger. I could feel the fidelity of the shop; I could sense the power of commitment flowing through their skills and mannerisms, and their lust for life and the sport was being zapped from them to me. I could feel their energy being harnessed, and at any given moment passing that energy on to the customer. Eventually one runs out of energy, but that was not detectable at the store.

The next few days were just unbelievable on the Raleigh; I got to break out of the walls and hit the streets. My first day out was, by far, my best day involved in a new hobby or a new sport. The shop was right on the money. I ventured out around 5 p.m., got through the first two neighborhoods and was just north of my house about three miles when I got my first taste of riding on the streets. I had my headphones on, and the shuffle clipped to my t-shirt. I had Iron Maiden blaring through the one earpiece so I could hear for cars and anything else that came my way. Seventeen miles was the smallest loop the shop had marked out, so seventeen miles I went. I rode past some beautiful properties and gorgeous homes that I had never seen before. I passed a few farms, passed over a few creeks, and I got to feel the lay of the land. Now, one thing that I never foresaw was the difference between the streets in my neighborhood and the real roads. My neighborhood had just laid down new asphalt and the roads were not as flat, or as absorbent as they had been over the last month. My body could feel every single bump, every single crack and uneven speck on the first ride out-I knew I had to do something about that. But, I was still in the early stages; I had not told anyone I was riding a thousand miles for charity yet. I had to understand firsthand that I could be committed to this vision before I would tell my family and friends. Sure, my wife knew about this, but that was it. I told her and she understood I had to feel confident that I could start and finish the job.

The next day was the worst my body had felt-my hands were throbbing, my butt was aching, my elbows were sore, my right knee was swollen and my lower back was feeling awkward-other than that I felt a sense of accomplishment. Seventeen miles out in the streets were in the books, it was yesterday's news. I knew I could do this once more, I knew I could put this sport in my hip pocket and carry out the mission. But it was going to take total commitment on my part; the bicycle shop was a guide, the bicycle was the equipment, but it was my determination that got me this far and was going to carry me all the way.

Mission statements are written and hung up all over the place and talked about every single day across the United States and throughout the world. The mission statement is a sign of total commitment, all in. It is not written and then put in the back room for another day, but is blasted on businesses' websites and walls, hung up on billboards, seen in magazines, on the backs of bottles, cans, or loaves of bread. Even peanut butter has a mission statement on the back of the jar.

Total commitment is how I see the bicycle shop. Here is what it says on their website: "…we believe that great people are the key to our success. Our employees are knowledgeable and friendly. Best of all, they all ride bicycles and love the sport of cycling. Although our store is beautiful and stocked with great products, our people are the best reason to visit us." (11) SOLID, SOLID commitment to people first, and the selling of products comes second. They understand that without one, the other is never achieved. This store is totally committed to me and the many thousands of customers who walk through their doors each month. The owner displays that notion every single time I go up there. The staff is friendly, but why? Because they want to be there, because they have a zest for cycling, and a zest for customer service. If you have never been in a bicycle shop, I suggest you venture up to your local shop and see what transpires there. They are usually limited on space. They are usually small and packed full of artillery for the bicycle scene and, unlike the huge mega supercenters, there is nowhere for employees to hide or avoid interacting with customers. They are the center of attention-to see this in motion is just unbelievable. The commitment one has to have in this high-energy establishment is unreal.

I researched a few other bicycle shops in the United States and below are a few noteworthy comments.

New Moon Ski and Bike-"The most important thing to all of us here at New Moon is customer service. Our knowledgeable staff works with customers to find the products that will help them have a great experience." (12)

Sugar's Bike Shop -"We will educate you and make sure you are getting the best bike for you."(13)

Buck's Bikes-"…30 years of quality bikes, accessories, and reliable service. Our experienced staff will be happy to find the perfect bike or gear to fit your family's style and needs."(14)

Sierra Bicycle Works-"We are a well-established shop with a long track record of honesty, integrity, and expertise."(15)

Cedar Bluff Cycles-"We constantly strive to offer quality service and expertise to exceed our customers' expectations and provide an enjoyable working environment to our employees."(16)

Riverfront Cycle- "Dedicated to providing you with honest, competent, reliable and quality service at an affordable price from an experienced and knowledgeable staff. Our commitment to excellence is only surpassed by our love of the sport."(17)

Now for the record, I have not been to a single one of these bicycle shops, nor do I know anyone who is employed by them. But what I find intriguing is the notion that all of them have one thing in common: the determination to provide quality service. Customers are funny people-one day they are in a good mood, but the next time we see them they may be in an awful mood. But, what never fails in the business is providing the customer quality service, something as simple as a hello with a name on the end, something so simple as asking how my daughter is doing, asking how my rides are going, asking me how my knees feel. It is a classic touch of customer service. I thoroughly enjoy the image of the barber shop; every single time it is shown on TV, the barber knows every single person who walks in the door, but on day one, the business had no clue who those customers were. They had to build the business from the bottom up.

I am sure a few haircuts were wrong, maybe the fade was a little short, the flat top was a little crooked, the Mohawk for the teenager was a little iffy, but by the second time it was right on the money. Why did the customer come back if the haircut was wrong? There was a little notion of personal touch that transpired there, a little glimmer of comfort came their way, so they returned for the same experience, which lead them there over and over and over again. That lead to them telling their friends and family, which lead them to tell their family and friends, and the cycle grew and grew and grew. Hugh was my barber all through grade school and high school. When my wife and I bought a new house, I had to switch barbers-Chuck was his name. He drove a Harley Davidson, and a pickup truck. He was a man's man in the business of giving haircuts. On day one, I knew I was in the right place. It just felt comfortable; he was down to earth, and there was nothing flashy about the place. No TVs, just a small radio in the corner, a few chairs, and a few magazines. But every single time I left, I had a quality haircut and a quality visit-that is what kept me going back over and over.

It is the same notion for the bicycle shops I listed above. When searching for a bicycle we have a choice to make; we can go to the mega supercenter, the big sporting goods store, order online, or we can go to the local shop. WE, the customers, have a choice to make, and with each transaction a service will be provided and another service will not be provided. Cheap-go online. Quality-go to the local bicycle shop. Mega supercenters are very convenient, and, let's face it, not every community will have a bicycle shop nor will the community down the road. But one thing is for sure, there is a shop close to your house and if not, at least go find one and see what I am talking about.

Commitment to a customer is the way the world revolves these days. We bait the line, we give a few tugs, we reel them in and we have them for life-we don't throw them back. Customers have a bigger choice the more technical our society becomes. It is so easy to buy a knock-off bicycle from China, or a new carbon fiber wheel from Mexico. Once we get the customer in the door, it is up to the business to get them to come back-one shot, one kill, as a sniper would say. But it is the same in the real world; it took years for the customer to walk in for the first time and we can make or break that experience.

Commitment means all in-we are all in it from the word GO! However big or however small a business, everyone has to be committed to their task in order for the outcome to be successful. The owner, GM, CEO, CFO, salesman, saleswomen, cashier, stock boy/girl, janitor, and even the part-time and holiday workers have to be sold on the notion of commitment. WE are all in this together and each transaction that takes place pays for this establishment to operate daily. Businesses work too hard and too long to lose a customer on the first go-round. On the flipside, some customers are hard to get along with. If a person walked into the bicycle shop and asked for a Giro Advantage 2 with Roc Loc 5 aero bicycle helmet and the store did not carry it, the customer may ask what kind is stocked. Most shops will offer an alternative, for example, we carry a Bell Javelin triathlon helmet or a Louis Garneau Chrono-Leggera aero helmet. The shop offers the customer a different variety than what they are looking for. Some may stick to their guns, having only wanted to purchase that type of helmet. The store offers alternate means of equipment and may even offer to order the helmet to appease the customer, but some may not stand for that and walk out never to return. Shops, like any other business, can't please every single customer, but they can offer another means or another outlet to ease the customers buying experience. Now, that is commitment.

# CHAPTER 7 EQUIPMENT

"Bicycling is a big part of the future. There's something wrong with a society that drives a car to work out in a gym."-Bill Nye the Science Guy

This is a titanic subject matter to look at carefully in any business- what equipment do we retail and make available to our patrons and our workforce? A ton of attention to detail, a heap of research, a mountain of sampling and, of course, a magnitude of trade shows are involved when weighing in on what to incorporate. However, anyone who opens a business has a knack for knowing what is in demand, what works well, what consumers require in the different seasons and, when they listen to the customers' requests and inquires, they provide what the trend demands.

Just in the bicycle community which entails road bikes, mountain bikes, commuter bikes, triathlon bikes, Time Trial, BMX bikes, cruiser bikes, youth bikes, women's bikes, hybrid bikes and more, the store has to make an assessment regarding which ones he/she is going to sell- which ones move and which ones collect dust. Collecting dust does not mean the bike does not sell well, it just means the bike is not doing well here in the local community. As the owner of the business, it is hard to tell a customer a particular item is not stocked, but it is in the store's best interest not to accumulate a wide range of items just hoping the right customer walks in the door to purchase it. Many nights, many days, and many hours have been spent researching what sells and what just sits. It is hard to determine what moves at first, it is hard to determine what customers need and love, but through trial and error, the store can simply understand the root of what will keep their stores open and thriving. The biggest payoff comes from listening to customers' needs, listening to their feedback, listening to their voices. As easy as it may be to listen, it could be a huge payoff, and economically sound. The customer knows what he/she wants-they could and will bring new concepts to any business and it is up the store to listen and listen well. As the saying goes, God gave us two ears and one mouth, therefore, we have to listen twice as much as we speak.

Equipment includes the hardware and accessories that come along with a task. Camping, for example, is a huge sport requiring many accessories, and many components are involved in this recreational and die-hard sport. The store I love is REI; years ago, I went to my first one in Anchorage, Alaska with my family. The space the store had was unbelievable. The selection of tools, tents, sleeping bags, hiking gear, shoes, boots, coats, helmets, climbing gear, hydration systems, dried food and nutrition, I, the customer, had to choose from was endless. A few years ago, REI opened its doors here in Indianapolis and, upon hearing that, I had to go. To describe the store as compared to the one in Alaska was easy to do. It is SMALL. Why is it small? Easy. How many mountain ranges are in Indiana? How many expeditions are going on in Indiana? How many episodes of The World's Deadliest Catch have been filmed here in this state? How many people are drilling for oil here in town? How many people are excavating for gold here in this state? It's pretty easy to answer those questions: not much at all. However, Indiana offers a vast array of outdoor activities ranging from hiking, bicycling, camping, and other outdoor activities. So the lesson here is, REI can still have a strong presence in the community, but they have to limit the hardware they carry to accommodate the needs of the community. Sure, they can order bear callers or a $700 pair of subzero hiking boots, but they don't carry them on the shelves. There is no need to tie up inventory or watch it collect dust, and the same goes for the local bicycle shop.

Some names of bicycle manufacturers are: Cannondale, SOTT, Giant, Trek, Schwinn, Mongoose, Diamondback, Specialized, Raleigh, Huffy, Gary Fisher, Ellsworth, Klein, Bianchi, GT, Haro, Fuji, Shimano, Jamis, Rocky Mountain, Pinarello, Ridley, and Eddy Merckx. Here is another way to look at equipment and why it so important to select the correct inventory for the store-and why it is so important to understand the equipment that is out there.

SCOTT, a world leader in bicycles, manufactures the following types of bikes and equipment:
1. Mountain-any trail, any time.
2. Contessa-for women who move.
3. Junior-for all rising stars.
4. Urban-color your city.
5. Trekking-explore and more.
6. E-bikes-arrive energetic.
7. Road-your next bike.
8. Footwear-perfect fit.
9. Helmets-always ahead.
10. Bags-tech bag, highest standard.
11. Eyewear-precision optics.
12. Bikewear-life is better in color.

The SCOTT mountain bike is pretty straightforward, a mountain bike. Okay, so you use it to climb a mountain, and it goes through mud well, I am sure. It is what my college and fraternity buddies all used, and the bikes all look pretty much the same, if you ask me. WRONG! That is what I thought before heading up to the bicycle shop. There the salesman told me how many different varieties of mountain bikes SCOTT manufactures. He handed me a brochure outlining what they offer.

The SPARK is a maximum traction bike and is suitable for everyday riders and endurance racers. The types they provide are: SPARK 900 SL, SPARK 900 PREMIUM, SPARK 900 RC, SPARK 910, SPARK 610, SPARK 920, SPARK 620, SPARK 930, SPARK 940, SPARK 640, SPARK 950, SPARK 650, SPARK 960, and SPARK 660. (18) That is a ton of varieties; the 900 series is a 29 inch frame and the 600 series is a 26 inch frame, and that is just on one type, the SPARK mountain bike. The next bike is the racing mountain bike, called the SCALE; this series runs eight different bikes and comes in 26 inch or 29 inch, so that is sixteen different bikes. The next bike is a trail bike called the GENIUS; this bike is for trail riding and it comes in eleven different types that range from 27 inch to 29 inch. The GAMBLER is simply a fast downhill, free-ride mountain bike, and it comes in three types. The VOLTAGE is a park and play type mountain bike which is geared for more park-style and slope-style riding; it comes in eleven different types. Last, but not least, there is the ASPECT, which is for the all-around rider. It comes in five different types and has a choice, once again, between a 26 inch and a 29 inch bike, a total of ten bikes in that series. All of those are for men only-there is a women's line as well. WOW, a great selection!

I have twelve sections dedicated to the types of equipment and accessories that SCOTT provides its customers, but the paragraph above only breaks down the mountain bike. As you can tell, that is a very extensive inventory for one bike, but over the years SCOTT has developed and produced an assortment to appeal to all types of mountain bikers. SCOTT, reminiscent of the bicycle shops across the United States and throughout the world, understands its equipment and identifies with the buying habits of the consumer. Could you imagine walking into a bicycle shop and seeing just the SCOTT mountain bikes on display? That would be very overwhelming and it would be a ton of inventory locked in under one roof. The shop is just like the salon, the coffee shop, or the local market; they have a slew of varieties and, at first, it is so hard to understand which ones to incorporate.

I worked at a little convenience store from age 16-21. The manager/owner was Earl Mette, a very fascinating man, very welcoming, very extroverted, and, of course, he had a potent business frame of mind. His prices were a little elevated compared to the supermarket, and his selection was, naturally, smaller than the supermarket, but he offered the community a fairly wide range of equipment and groceries. You could buy a frozen pizza, olive oil, baby food, canned beans, diced onions, fresh bananas, coffee and more. The store was minuscule, but it could deliver concrete effectiveness. The place was always swarming day and night, and two cashiers were essential, manning their battle stations from sunup to sundown. The store was always jumping and full of liveliness. Most of the guys I worked with were around my age. The owner, Earl, had two sons, Brian and Kevin, both of whom brought balance to the force. One was a go-getter during the day, and the other ran the store at night; both understood their responsibilities and carried them out with aptitude. I recall the mail coming in and the mounds of magazines full of new equipment and new varieties offered to the convenience store market. I remember getting Stadium Club baseball cards in, the ones with high definition photos on the card. They were selling like hotcakes, we could not keep them in stock. Upon seeing the first two boxes sold in under a week, Kevin purchased over 100 boxes of them and kept them under lock and key near the cash register. Within a few months, they had all been sold, and dollar signs were flashing in front of Kevin's eyes. He monitored his store, he understood what was selling and what was hot for the moment, and he did not skip a beat. The store was surrounded by a thousand homes, the largest subdivision at the time in the state of Ohio, and his store was right in the middle of it-location, location, location-boy, did it ever pay off.

The success of the convenience store was due to this: the owners understood equipment, and they supplied what the consumers desired. It was a win-win situation. Like the bicycle shop, they had to comprehend supply and demand. They needed to learn firsthand from their suppliers what was hot off the press, and what was being phased out. Cannondale, another bicycle manufacturer, offers an extensive selection, ranging, once again, from mountain bike, urban bike, specification bike, and road bike. With the road bike, like the one that I am using on the journey of 1000 miles, I am sure it is difficult to stockpile a multitude of items in the expectation that they all will sell. Here in the Midwest we have four seasons: spring, summer, fall, and winter. Unlike Florida, Arizona, and southern California, we don't have good weather year round. We get snow, subzero temperatures, and wind-chill. But none of that precludes being smart in business; we adapt and we overcome and we adjust just like the Marine Corps does. Nothing is free, and there are no free rides in any business. Sure, there are breaks, but through evaluating the surrounding environment the game is played and won.

The Cannondale road bike comes in four different types-elite road, performance road, triathlon/TT and cyclo-cross. Now here is where it gets tricky once again; there are twenty different varieties of elite road, eleven types of performance road, six types of triathlon/TT, and eight types of cyclo-cross. That is forty-five types of bikes in one category, so if forty-five people walked into the store and asked for forty-five different Cannondale road bikes, the store would be in heaven. But we all know that will never materialize. It is not realistic to stock all forty-five types of bikes and have four of each at the ready, a total of 180 types of bikes.

Having the precise equipment means having product knowledge-it means understanding the lay of the land, understanding the seasons, understanding buying habits, understanding the needs of the customers. The leader, as I mentioned earlier, has got to understand they are in the business of selling bicycles, however, they are not in the business of tying up inventory and stockpiling items that just will not sell. Even if four sold in one week, that in no way necessitates ordering 100 of them, for they may never sell again. A cycling team may have bought them all, or a grandma bought them for the grand kids for Christmas. But as the leader of the pack, the store clerks should be able to relay that information back to the owner on why they sold; that is the payoff on the circuit of open communication inside the business circle.

In the movie Butch Cassidy and the Sundance Kid, a smiling Paul Newman is seen riding a bicycle in the fields with a lovely girl standing on the back. It is a stunning setting in a rather tough old western movie, but it shows the softer side of the main character. It shows him taking the time to enjoy life, it shows him being human and having a connection with another person. It is an all too familiar message in the bicycle world: have fun, enjoy life, and go out and see the world. The world is huge, but for one moment, the movie nailed it. The bicycle is a means of transportation; it is a means for commuting, for getting ice cream, and for carrying items. The bicycle company Electra understands that concept of the movie, and they take pride in delivering that message to its customers. Electra is a manufacturer of what is commonly known as the cruiser bike; this is the bike we ride along the beach with our family, to the grocery store to get milk, and we can ride it to work and not have to change clothes. This is the bike with the comfy seat, and the back rack to place our computer or any other item and it will stay put.

The bicycle shop that I have been going to takes pride in understanding the equipment needed to keep their doors open; it can't just be about velocity or performance. Bicycles are expanding and escalating as

## CHAPTER 7 EQUIPMENT

we talked about previously. Bicycling is excellent for the environment, a great means of fitness, and a wonderful way to see the countryside. But not everyone will be looking for the triathlon bike, nor will they be looking for a cyclo-cross bike. Understanding customers and awareness of the community is how the store opts for their equipment astutely. He/she must comprehend all clients are different. The Electra bicycle is an excellent example of our shifting world. Electra gets it and they are running with it. They supply over thirty-seven different styles of bikes accommodating adults, youth, and children.

Just like any other business, we have to offer customers a variety of what we think is the finest, what is trending, and also throw in a few new state of the art technologies. But as a customer, I saw myself as a person with a huge question mark over my head every single time I stepped into the store-I felt lost. I felt overwhelmed. Despite all of that, the one common theme is I felt comfortable going up there, I knew I was in good hands. I knew the shop was looking out for me, and for my best interests. So here I am riding a road bike-are the same principles offered to an enthusiast of a mountain bike, or a cruiser? I would like to respond to that question with an emphatic YES. I often observe the staff engaging the customers with equipment; I witness their broad smiles while helping each individual with equipment purchases, which in turn keeps the customer's vision alive. I observe them explaining the benefits of each piece of equipment like a docent would explain an exhibit in the Smithsonian. They are, in reality, tour guides who take us on a visual tour across the store; they illustrate, explain, and converse with us each model's capabilities.

Here is a list of a few bicycle components: chains, front and rear derailleur's, brake calipers and brake pads, cassettes, cranks, chain rings, bottom brackets, headsets, shifters and brake levers, skewers, hubs, hub bodies, bearings and forks. To compile a list of all the companies who manufacture these components would take forever, so I will share with you one company who takes on this challenge and does it skillfully. The corporation is SRAM. (19) In this state of the art company they share, "Bike components are all we do, which is why we do them so mind-bendingly well." Now imagine this, all the bicycles that I listed earlier and not a single one was called SRAM. SRAM is not a bicycle manufacturer; they make the nuts and bolts of the bicycle itself. They make the "rider appreciate solid performance, reliability, dependability and all the standard qualities one would expect." SRAM products are carried at the bicycle shop, and the young men and women have hats, t-shirts, stickers and coffee mugs displaying the SRAM logo. But advertisement does not just sell a product, it pushes it to the front, but people still have got to repeatedly purchase it to bring the creation to fruition. SRAM-I never heard of it till I began bicycling, never once heard it mentioned at all until I dove into the sport of cycling. Now I am educated on the brand because the store was educated on the brand. This brand has many faces in the crowd, such as SRAM RED, SRAM FORCE, SRAM RIVAL, and SRAM QUARQ. The company states, "We will continue to seek and deploy technology and engineering advancements, as we compulsively refine and redefine the pinnacle of the ultimate ride."

Now here we are talking about another bicycle part, and once again I feel overwhelmed just looking at what I am typing –bicycling has a mammoth, vast array of equipment. It has countless companies competing for a stronghold in a fast growing sport and it is up to the bicycle shop to carry these items. It is also in the bicycle shop's best interest to carry what it must, and to educate their staff and customers as to what equipment is necessary, and what is not. There is a difference in buying a bicycle-is it for commuting, is it for racing, is it for a triathlon competition? The bicycle shop has it all, and if they don't, they will get it in, I am sure. As we walk through this chapter of the book, I want to look at all the inventory that a store has to carry, and I want you to decide if it is worth it. Tires are pretty straightforward. Okay, which ones do you carry? Continental, TUFO, Vittoria, Maxxis, Michelin, Zipp, Geax. Now onto the wheels-which ones do you carry? Zipp, HED, Mavic, Shimano. Which brands of cycling gear do you carry? Castelli, Pearl Izumi, Louis Garneau, 2XU, DeSoto, Craft, Zoot, TriSports. Now onto nutrition-no bike shop is complete without it. So what do you incorporate? Bars, gels, drinks, and supplements all have suppliers competing to get in your store and here are a few names: Hammer, Powerbar, Clif, ProBar, First Endurance, Honey Stinger, SportQuest, Gatorade, Nuun, Pacific, Cytomax, SaltStick, INFINIT, Champion, Extreme Endurance, Fluid Recovery, and many more. Last are the accessories-these are the little items that complete the mission. Once again, there are many manufacturers of these little items-ointments, magnets, saddle covers, inflation kits, massage balls, tape, CO2, bike pumps, lights, reflectors, skewers, valve extenders, bar end plugs, speed box, wheel bags, tool bags, patch kits, cements, batteries, hydration systems, and more. Just on hydration systems alone there are TorHans, Xlab, Camelback and Arundel-which lead to the types of systems, there are profile, speed fill, water bottles, water bottle cages, rear and front mount systems and ZIPP speed cages.

When I was finished with the previous day's ride, my body was in shock-I took on a few hills, took on the cracks in the road and my butt really ached, my elbows were painful and I had to do something about it. My wife and I negotiated that once I broke out of the neighborhood, I could purchase a cycling jersey and cycling shorts, the ones with the padding underneath, to help absorb the impact. Sure enough I got a pair-and I was officially in the game -the bike, the outfit and the shop. This mission was looking solid.

# CHAPTER 8 KNOWLEDGE

"An investment in knowledge pays the best interest."- Benjamin Franklin

With the last chapter dealing with equipment, I knew the next one had to deal with knowledge-knowledge is power. Teachers ask kids to read books, practice their handwriting each day, and the payoff is that the children's education will benefit them by landing them a place in a distinguished college, a better job, a healthier understanding of the community in which they live, sharp social skills, and, of course, much higher self-esteem.

Knowledge is the greatest aptitude a person can expand, in business and for personal gratification. It is what sets people and businesses apart. People are grouped all the time by their knowledge. Just look on any application- GED, high school, college-associate's, bachelors, masters, doctorate. It is not wrong to get an understanding of a person's background-however the yearning for knowledge must never cease. Imagine where our society would be if we failed to gain additional education, stopped trying to find more answers to questions. E=MC2 never would have been comprehended, nor would we have been able to find a cure for polio. The question that arises is, when do you stop learning? The answer is never. At work, at home, at church, at school we have to keep knowledge afloat in order to stay current and stay challenged in our society. Those who think good things will come based on just their names are fooling themselves-the business who operates on the notion I have had my door open for fifty years will get eaten alive by his/her competition.

Learning never takes a time-out -if we take it easy, the competition will outdo us, and who wants that. Knowledge is shared from within companies and shared with patrons all the time. Knowledge is why clients keep coming back; they know they will have the best quality interaction, the best state of the art tools and amenities available. My wife and I are now on our fourth house, having been married for thirteen years as of this writing. We have utilized only two real-estate agencies. One was in Cincinnati for the purchase of two houses, and one was here in Indiana buying the other two houses. The first one was really straightforward, we used the identical company that my parents had used in the past. The second group is FC Tucker. When transitioning from Cincinnati to Indianapolis, my wife and I had no clue as to who to use, when a friend of ours recommended his niece. Her personal skills, communication skills, and work ethic were of the highest quality and she landed us our first house on the first day we visited with her.

A few years later, we decided to move north of Indianapolis to the city of Carmel-we asked if she would sell our house and, of course, she was happy to. A few weeks after listing the house, she was killed in a tragic auto accident by a drunk driver. My wife and I were completely devastated upon hearing of her passing; she was a kindhearted woman, a caring person, beautiful woman, top- notch mom and a great ambassador to the real-estate community. We decided to take our house off the market. A co-worker heard of our decision and said, "I know this magnificent representative that could do wonders for you and your house. Give him a buzz and he will take the reins and deliver exactly what you need." Not knowing what to do, we took our friends counsel and gave the agent a call. In less than thirty days, we sold our residence for the asking price, and then landed a new house. In thirty days, our house sold and we had a new address. Stuff like that does not just happen overnight- it does not just occur because he was kind to us, nor does it occur in the current housing market. But our agent knew what he was doing; he was knowledgeable about the vicinity in which we lived-close to the city, golf course atmosphere-and he knew where we wanted to move and made the transition as smoothly as possible. Word of mouth got us that sale, word of mouth got the agent two houses, and word of mouth created a partnership for years to come. Why? That is clear-cut; the co-worker had a similar encounter with this agent, and he shared his perception with us, which then lead to the agent using his astuteness to selling and buying us a house. Houses sit on the market for days and days or even months-but this agent sold our house in less than thirty days. Piece of cake to him-but here are the reasons why.

1. Graduated from high school 1984
2. Graduated from college 1988
3. Member of Phi Gamma Delta Fraternity
4. Proctor and Gamble 1988-1992
5. Buying agent of the year 1996
6. Listing agent of the year 1997
7. Top Ten sales for F.C. Tucker 1994-present
8. Lifetime President Club member 1994-present
9. Marketing excellence award for most sold listings and buyers combined 1999-2001
10. Marketing listing award for most listings sold 2004
11. Realty Alliance Award 2005-2012
12. Executive sales club, over 8 million sold 2005-2012
13. Leading Sales producer 2008
14. Indianapolis top 50 realtors 2008-present

Okay-since we are looking at this together, what would you say about this inventory? Is it impressive, is it overwhelming, is it too long, is it too short, or do you say who cares? The answer is in the following statement that sets this agent on the top shelf.

"He strives to provide professionalism beyond reproach and integrity without compromise. His amazing energy level is fueled by a passion and commitment to provide unsurpassed levels of personalized service. One of his goals is to keep the transaction as worry free as possible. His exceptional negotiating ability enables him to obtain the best results for you." (20)

This man, this agent, did not just wake up one day and say look at what I have obtained-he woke up every single day and cultivated himself on his surroundings. Indianapolis is a titanic city, with booming suburbs, and it is very, very competitive among real-estate agents. Just drive around and peek at all of the for sale signs in your community and see all the different names on the signs; it is a very complicated and time consuming profession-Monday through Sunday. But the file above is not awarded to those who linger; it is rewarded to those who go after. Knowledge of the occupation, knowledge of the community and knowledge of work ethic, intelligent direction, wise choices and skillful execution are what makes this agent top notch. F.C. Tucker, the agency the agent works for, understands that agents are only as brilliant as the agency that supports them. Laws change, buying habits change, communities change, and the agency has to be knee deep in the power of knowledge needed to excel at being competitive in an always aggressive environment. When we list our house again, we will go with him, and to this day, I inform people all about him. His rap sheet is filled in, but he still goes out and challenges himself to gain brainpower. He is at the top for a reason-he exemplifies customer service, and he is committed to his peers, his agency, and to his profession.

In the competitive world of bicycling, the buying practices are changing everything-online, direct warehouse, and so on. I want you to envision a bicycle and all the components that come with it-the tires, spokes, pedals, chainring, cluster, set, handlebar, brakes, frame, stem, derailleur, chain, crank arm, forks, hubs, rims and shifters. Now this is where it gets tricky-you order the bicycle from a website, and you saved a few hundred dollars; great, I am all for savings, who isn't? But this is the real risky part. What do you do if the bike is not shifting properly after you ride it one time? Who do you call? Do you pack it up and ship it back? Do you just ride it, not knowing what is wrong and hope it works its way out? On the subject of shifting alone, there are over 100 possible reasons a bike won't shift, and I will list a few.

1. Crack or split in cable housing-possibly under the ferrule where it can't be seen.
2. Crack in the barrel adjuster.
3. Dirt inside the adjuster.
4. Worn bottom bracket bearings.
5. Loose chainring bolts.

##### CHAPTER 8 KNOWLEDGE    **107**

6. Bent B axle.
7. Bent P axle.
8. Bent hub axle.
9. Crack in cog.
10. Chainring installed backwards.

These are ten-now add ninety more reasons why the bike will not shift appropriately. One hundred reasons, 100 headaches, 100 setbacks to you going out and hitting the road, 100 reasons to get infuriated, 100 reasons to get frustrated, 100 reasons to blame the bike and exchange it and buy another one. The power of knowledge is just unbelievable in the scheme of things. Knowledge leads to sales, customer satisfaction, and to a turnstile operation. The bicycle shop next to my house is just that-sure they don't necessarily know immediately how to handle every single circumstance that walks in the door, but they know how to reference that thought and come up with a logical solution quickly. The knowledge that they are provided by the team leader/owner is what sets this place apart from its counterparts. This atmosphere is going on in thousands of bicycle shops across the country and across the world.

Sixty days into the journey, sixty days without revealing to anyone what was going on, I knew that I was all in. I knew the shop's knowledge had gotten me this far, for I had logged 577 miles of training. I had been to the shop a dozen times over the course of the journey and I had one more obstacle to conquer. If I could do my first century ride-100 miles- then I would allow people to know what I was doing. A hundred miles in one day, on sixty days of training, I knew then that the shop, my family, and friends could all be told what I was doing. It was not intended to be a secret, but I still did not even tell my friend who I was riding to Florida for that I was 100% committed yet. All he knew was the vision was alive and well-but I explained to him I had to see if my body could handle it. I ventured up to the shop and gathered a few items for the ride-my bottles were full of crud, so I purchased new ones. The salesman, Brian, the man who I saw on day one asked how I was doing. I told him I was heading for 100 miles tomorrow and he proceeded to tell me good luck. He said, "You WILL do it, you are ready. Take your time and just hit the 100 mark, don't worry about time-just finish it." He knew I was not racing, he understood the desire I had to complete the ride, and he said, "You are going to nail it. Just drink plenty of water and eat and eat some more."

I was up and at 'em at 6 a.m. and on the streets at 8 a.m. after three bowls of cereal and plenty of water. I did a thirty-six mile pass with no problem, stopped at the house for a potty break, filled up the bottles, had a ham sandwich, then back at it. This time, I did the thirty mile loop, and my body was starting to feel it. I hit the house again, ate another sandwich, filled the bottles and then I did the seventeen mile loop. At this point, my butt was killing me, my arms felt like Jell-O, my knees felt great. My neck was tingling and my arms were getting red-sunburn. My gloves were soaking wet, the bottoms of my feet were sore-I felt my feet slipping off the pedals. My stomach muscles were hurting, but my mind felt great-I had listened to three quarters of all the songs on my shuffle and right before I headed back home, the shuffle died. I was at eighty-three miles when I hit the house again-I had seventeen miles to go. I was confident, but I was a little concerned that if I hit the loop and passed out that I would be far from home, so I did the last seventeen miles in the neighborhood. Back and forth I went-no music, just me and the street. Back and forth I went, and it seemed like it took forever; my speed at that moment had to be ten miles per hour. I was exhausted, but by 4 p.m. I had my first century ride in the books, 100 miles. When I got back to the house, I ate another ham sandwich and drank water and more water. I stretched and stretched and took a thirty minute hot shower, got dressed, and I headed up to the Mexican restaurant and ate a burrito and drank diet coke-I must have had ten of them. My wife and little girl were in Cincinnati that day, so I had planned the day well. A hundred miles I kept saying, repeating it over and over. I called my wife, I called my parents, and of course, the next day I had to go to the shop and inform them.

Okay, this is where I get schooled in the knowledge department by the bicycle shop. I walked in after work, and proceeded to tell them I had done the century ride. They were all overwhelmed at the joy I had with this accomplishment, and I thanked them for helping me get this far-they proceeded to ask where I went, what I ate. I told them a ham sandwich and water. "HAM SANDWICH," said the big guy. "Are you crazy? That will tear you up." He asked how many sandwiches I ate, and when I told him three, he said, "Are you nuts!" With that, all the staff huddled around me, breaking out in little laughs, yet a bit concerned with my eating habits. The big guy proceeded to explain that my body cannot break down that food fast enough to convert it into energy. He said the sandwich just sits in your stomach and waits and waits to break down-way too long for the energy I needed for the ride. The others jumped in and started asking if I had been drinking any electrolytes. "Electro what?" I asked. They laughed again; they saw me all in the sport, but they needed to share eating habits with me. Eating habits 101-I felt like a freshman at college, all in but a little adrift. But all of them took me under their wing and introduced me to the nutritional side of biking. They took me over to the Hammer Nutrition (21) stand and talked about the benefits of these items, and the big guy told me to come to the back and talk once I was done looking at the products. They showed me the array of products: Hammer Gels, Hammer Recoverite, Hammer Heed, Hammer Sustained Energy, Hammer Whey, Hammer Soy, Hammer Bars-all the essential nutrition I needed to stay hydrated and focused on this journey. They explained the salt lost and salt intake and what electrolytes do. Hammer Nutrition has been in the supplement business for over two decades; this company produces high-quality supplements and takes the guess work out of two components, fueling and supplementation. WOW-here I have been an athlete for 42 years, and not once did I have a clue as to what I needed for my body. The bicycle shop's knowledge was creating a whole new side to the sport-they ALL were looking out for me.

Knowledge is power. In an article from About.com, (22) an excellent site on many topics, Shari Waters writes a passage about the Benefits of Product Knowledge; she states "Knowledge is power and for retailers, product knowledge can mean more sales. It is difficult to effectively sell to a customer if we cannot show how a particular product will address a shopper's needs." She goes on to describe the many benefits of knowing the product retailers sell. She notes that knowledge strengthens communications skills, boosts enthusiasm, grows confidence, and assists in overcoming objections. Product knowledge is amazing; it is what I would consider the biggest asset to maintaining customers. I have been to many stores, outlets, malls, restaurants, movie theaters, and etc. Then again, who hasn't? We always remember the moment we arrive. Was the ticket taker nice, the teller outgoing, the waiter kind, the cashier polite? There are two major grocery stores within a half mile of my house. One is on the right side of the road, and one is on the left side of the road. I have a choice to make. Each time I go to the one on the right they are so kind and they have every single thing I need.

The same goes for the one on the left, every single time they, as well, fill the void I am looking for. So what separates them? MILK and that is it. Both stores have the milk in the dairy section way back in the corner, hoping that you will pick up a few items on the way back or on the way to the checkout line. But, the store on the right has a little dairy section right as you enter the store-just a small case of milk for easy in and out. Yes, knowledge is thriving in the two stores; however, something as simple as a smaller dairy case at the front can get me in and out of the store fast. Now, imagine a mother with three kids who only needs two gallons of milk-she can come right in grab two and head out the door. How did they know to do that? Knowledge, because of their understanding that milk is a huge seller. If it is convenient for the customer, we may get them to buy more items, or they will remember we can get them in and out quickly to fill their needs.

Expertise is a way of understanding knowledge-he or she is an expert in their field of study. As we look at a professor, we understand they are an expert-they study, analyze, critique, lecture, and have the ability (in most cases) to bring their passion, their wisdom of the subject to the classroom. The same goes for every single person working out in the world. We are the professors, we are the leaders in our field of work-the person with whom we are engaging in conversation will, within a few minutes, understand we are sharp and educated on the subject, or they will realize we are full of mumbo jumbo. The bicycle shop is just the classroom, the showroom floor. There are tons of labels, colors, manufacturers, gadgets, clothes, and so forth to choose from. The sales clerk, mechanic, and owner of the shop understand that they have got to be prepared to handle a wide range of customers. Their instruction, the science, the craftsmanship of the shop must be of the highest standards across the land.

As I look at a picture of Lincoln, I see a man full of wisdom and full of education. When I walk into the bicycle shop I see the same qualities in the staff. On day one, I had no clue, it was just the first go-round-but day one grabbed me and pulled me in. The young man talking about the bicycles was Lincoln to me. His product knowledge is what I needed, he set the tone of the shop and ever since then they have never let me down. For the record, I am not a professional racer, nor do I own a $15,000 bike. My buying habits are very different from the group we see at the Ironman, SRAM, or Kona competitions. I am just a guy who has a vision of riding a bicycle to Florida for a cause. I am not looking to increase my speed, decrease my wind resistance, or buy booties to slip over my shoes for cold days of training-I am the guy just learning to understand the sport and how I can jump right in and enjoy it.

Gaining an array of knowledge on any subject is time consuming, daunting, and takes effort. Effort is what separates the do's from the do not's. It is effort to read about new equipment, it is effort to teach someone how to change a tire, a tube or change a pedal. It is effort on a slow day to take advantage of the time and tackle a new project that one is unfamiliar with. Sitting on the sidelines and hoping you will get in the game is not how one achieves that goal; practice, timeless effort, timeless courage, doing the little things, doing the simple things, and practicing what you believe in is how we win the game of business. That is what is occurring in bicycle shops, grocery stores, fashion malls, restaurants, theme parks, and etc. If you want to stay at the top, you have to continue to study.

The bicycle shop's product knowledge is on display 24/7, and customers of all shapes and sizes go up there for their knowledge of bicycles. I have one question for you-what is the difference between a squirrel and turkey? If you answered one can climb a tree and the other is for Thanksgiving, then you are correct. But in terms of riding a bicycle, a squirrel is an unstable rider who can't maintain a steady line and a turkey is an inexperienced rider. Now those two names are pretty common among any sport--he is squirrelly, he is a real turkey. But in terms of knowledge, those are the two types of customers I believe this shop loves to tackle head-on. They know the best of the best can ride with the best, and they know many riders can tackle a straight line, but it is the newbies like ME that they want to cultivate and foster a love of the sport. Fred and Doris are the two names used by seasoned veterans to describe newbies. I do literally look like a Fred-5 feet 10 inches, 242 pounds-or more like a Clydesdale.

Two words describe the shop's core, acumen and acuity. Acumen means keenness of a person's mind, and acuity means keenness the person displays. Keenness is a quick and penetrating intelligence according to the dictionary; it also is a positive feeling of wanting to push ahead and having a sharp edge. Those two words wholeheartedly describe my experience with this shop, but I am not alone, for others in our community that frequent the shop experience that, as well.

After gaining the facts of the nutritional side of the biking world, I scooted on back to the mechanics bay. There was the big guy, and when I say big, I mean enormous -his hands were so big, I think he could palm two basketballs. He proceeded to introduce himself as BIG Chris, for little Chris worked back there as well. He said, "I have been seeing you come up here all the time, and not once have I had a conversation with you, and we proceeded to chat. We talked about me just beginning the activity, we talked about where I live, where I ride and, of course, what he does. This gentle giant was a huge mountain biker-Nevada, North Carolina, Brown County in Indiana-this man loved mountain biking. For one hour we discussed, talked, and chitchatted about biking on a broad-spectrum. He said stay with it, you are going to love this sport. At one point he asked, "You did your first century ride in less than sixty days-why are you pushing yourself so hard? I looked around and said, "I am riding from Indiana to Florida." WHAT!!!!! He looked at me and said, "Going from nothing to Florida!" Big eyes came over me and him at the same time-we looked at each other-he knew I was all in, and I knew from his expressions he was all in the vision. He said, "You came to the right place. We all love biking, we love helping customers reach their goal for the season, or for the year, we all love what we do. One thing that stood out that day is his passion and commitment to the store and to his fellow employees. He told me with the utmost confidence that all the staff is conversant. I can question anyone about anything and they will be willing to rally around me. He laughed and said today was a great example. He was right. ALL helped.

# CHAPTER 9 COMMUNICATION

"In many ways, effective communication begins with mutual respect, communication that inspires, encourages or instructs others to do their best."-Zig Ziglar

The next week, I sat down with my wife and we went over the next stage of my vision. I explained to her that I felt I could do the trip. She looked at me and said, "GO FOR IT." After getting her support, I shot my friend in Orlando an email and explained what I had done thus far, and that I could make the journey-he, as well, said "GO FOR IT." At this point, I had 502 miles of training under my belt. I was getting into the thick of things-I knew I had to push myself harder and harder, yet keep my balance and stay the course. At this point, it was August 2, 2012, and I still had a few months to go. That night, I set the date for the journey to begin-I would leave on October 20th-my dad's birthday and the day after my daughter turned eight years old. I planned the route out through Google maps and the distance was 1033 miles from my house in Carmel, Indiana to Amway Center, the home of the Orlando Magic in Orlando, Florida. Looking at the map I could see hills, mountains, farms, cities, major and small, highways, side streets, country roads; all of those came into play when mapping out my journey. It was an overwhelming moment, and I started to think twice about it. One thousand thirty-three miles, am I crazy!!! But I knew it was for a good cause, and I was in the first-class hands of the SHOP, and that put my mind at ease.

Hello: a word so small, yet so powerful. It is the simplest gesture on the planet, yet so many of us have a hard time saying this elegant little word. We find it hard to engage with a person we don't know, yet we work in a business that depends on people. Why is it so hard to say hello? Is it because we have to say it first, or is it that we are shy and intimidated? I would say a little of both. For years, the communication of a handshake was the way to go, followed up by a hello. But in today's high-tech society with texting and emails at the forefront, I see many people getting further and further away from the human side of communicating-behind the phone, behind the emails, behind the texting it is so simple, but in public they are as nervous as a leaf on a tree. Shaking, stumbling, voice cracking, nothing is coming out, brain-dead, mute, and the list goes on-give them a keyboard and a speaker, and I am sure they could communicate just fine. Then on the complete flipside, I see the ones who are on the front burner, the ones making an effort to talk one- on-one and the payoff is literally huge. They are landing the jobs, getting the lead roles, getting the deal sealed, getting second interviews; they are climbing the ladder of success, returning customers, returning investors. Why? They can communicate, and converse with effectiveness.

Communication is a very simple approach in the business world, yet sometimes it is one of the hardest tasks to do. If one cannot communicate, then one's vision will fall by the wayside. Communicate so that employees and customers understand. Communicate with hope, optimism, motivation, and inspiration. Most of all, communicate publicly, for all to see, not behind closed doors. Make it known what you are doing; make it known how to excel at achieving customer service. Writing it down, talking about it, keeping the concept afloat is how battles and missions are won. Keeping it hidden, and not sharing the details can take a business down. Navy Seals are great at this; they practice, and practice, rehearse and rehearse before they tackle any mission. They know the ins and outs, they see the big picture and they communicate

## CHAPTER 9 COMMUNICATION 115

and talk, share and listen, then go out and hit the ground running and the vision is a success. We can learn a lot from the Seals, but in business we are the General Pattons. We must communicate all the time, every day. Communication is our friend, and we should incorporate it, treasure it, and use it to our advantage. Ronald Reagan got the Berlin Wall to come down with effective communication; imagine what you can do.

My first day at the bicycle shop was just like any other day to me-I was on a mission. The same goes for the shop; it was a walk in the park. The only thing that separated the store and me was the initial first contact. I walked in, head high, and with enthusiasm that day. The store, as well, seeing a new face had to step up their tenaciousness. But in retrospect, I feel that is who they were, and who they are. They are a communication center which happens to sell bicycles. The bicycle shop, as of March 2015, is ten years old, the same age as my little girl, Maggie. You don't achieve anniversaries of this magnitude by sitting back and waiting for others to take the first step; you get this far by taking the lead and driving it home.

Communication in any business has to thrive; it has to be the core of the program. Ideas are created, topics are generated and by sharing these with others, and allowing employees and customers to grow, businesses flourish and continue to grow at a great economic rate. Imagine the best bicycle in the world. Picture it: the tires, the seat, the frame, the spokes, the forks, the pedals, the chain, the crank. Okay, now picture your favorite amusement park ride: the steep climb and the quick descent, the sharp turns, and the rolling hills at lightning speed. The two are totally different, but the concept is the same. In order to become a ride or a bike, something had to take place behind the scenes; That is, the idea had to be shared to make an object of this proportion. Big, eventful visions are created every single day, however, the ones that do well are done well through constant communication. Round tables around the world are hard at work, handling the meetings of thousands of businesses. The table is just that, an object, but what takes place in meetings is a chance to be open with communication and share ideas and thoughts to formulate a healthier enterprise.

Zappos-if you have never heard of them, I suggest stop reading and log into zappos.com. Zappos.com is an excellent online store-it excels at selling clothing, shoes and numerous other items and is one of the frontrunners in a highly competitive market. What is unique about Zappos is that they have core values from which they develop culture, brand and business strategies.

The ten core values are as follows:
1. Deliver WOW through service.
2. Embrace and drive change.
3. Create fun and a little weirdness.
4. Be adventurous, creative, and open-minded.
5. Pursue growth and learning.
6. Build open and honest relationships with communication.
7. Build a positive team and family spirit.
8. Do more with less.
9. Be passionate and determined.
10. Be humble.

All ten core values set Zappos on the top shelf, and all ten are on display all the time. I have purchased a few things from this company over the years, and I have never been dissatisfied with my order. They continue to escalate, and continue to excel at their values day in and day out. The one entry on the list that really stands out is the sixth paragraph. Build open and honest relationships with communication. Looking at the list, you can identify that all ten are incorporated into one business; one value omitted and the business is slow-moving, keep all ten in the grasp and, watch out world, here they come. Zappos strives at all ten day in and day out, they never release one value nor build one way up-they steady the course so that they are even-keeled at their core values.

Zappos is just like all businesses in the world-they are striving to be number one in their designated fields. However, the difference among the great, the good, the average, and the sub-par is the sheer guts of communicating. Communicating the vision, communicating the changes, communicating among the employees, who then communicate to the customers, who then relay that information off to their friends and colleagues. To me, communicating is by far the biggest asset to accommodate any business. Without it, everything we are working for will come to a complete standstill. All employees of the bicycle shop are taking me from nothing to something-they are the project managers, and they don't even blink an eye at holding that responsibility. They are building me up; they are assembling me, as well as all the customers who are walking in the door. The interaction, which encompasses the vision, balance, commitment, partnership, knowledge, and equipment, is assembling each customer into one lean, mean, fighting machine. I felt sometimes as if I were a kindergartner in school when I headed up there-they were the teacher and I was the student. But that is the relationship I had with them; that relationship would later lead me to the finish line.

As I kept up with the training after a few days, I ran into my next door neighbor Scott Golden-Scott is a forty-two-year old guy, who owns his own business, plays racquetball five times a week before work, and plays in an over-forty baseball league. Scott is a go-getter, both personally and professionally. I was contemplating over the last week if it would be safe to do this ride by myself-I knew it would be more fun and enjoyable to go along with a friend and make the mission a team mission, for the bike shop taught me so much about teamwork. Scott's son and my daughter are buddies, always playing in the front yard, slip and slides or just throwing the football around. Scott and I had gotten to know each other pretty well over the last two years, and I knew he would be up for this challenge. On August 10, 2012, I asked Scott if he would join me in the quest. He looked at me and said, "WHAT! Ride a bike to Florida?" He then asked me to give him a few days to think it over. The next day, he stopped by and said, "I am all in." ALL IN-that means he had seventy days to train and prepare for this journey, plus he had had a knee operation only four months ago. But he was in great shape, and he felt confident in this journey. I communicated the vision of riding for charity, the four causes and how we can help make a difference in people's lives-he loved the idea, he loved the concept and, most of all, and he loved the challenge.

While I was writing this book, I stopped up at the shop one day to drop off some cookies my wife had made. While I was there, new ZIPP wheels came in. The store was filled with the fresh line of equipment for the 2013 season, and crammed with employees that day. They knew the shipment of goods was there to tackle, to get them out of the boxes and up on the shelves. When they opened the innovative equipment, all eyes were bright with anticipation of seeing the hardware being removed. Once removed by a member of the staff, I asked what the item was. Without any hesitation, he held up the new wheels and began to speak. As he spoke, a few customers and I scooted over to pay attention to him explain what they were. Then just like in kindergarten, the entire staff came over to listen in and fill in details. With great passion and the purest of heart, he went on for about fifteen minutes providing information about the history and the manufacturer of the new wheel. He was highly educated on ZIPP, but more importantly, he was communicating with his fellow employees and customers on the subject matter. He was the teacher, and we were his students. I felt just like a school kid, all huddled around the teacher as she read us a book. I was mesmerized by his demeanor and his ability to communicate his job to us. If that day were a tryout for a Broadway play, he would have nailed it- he displayed no hesitation, hiccups, or setbacks-his audition was off the charts. Earlier, I talked about the encore effect and that was another moment on why customers return; it was so simple, it came so natural and that moment I knew this place was a gem.

After getting the ALL GO, I had to get cycling shoes, and I had to get my clip-in pedals back on. One thing I explained to them was that my feet kept slipping. Little Chris told me to bring the bike up to get the pedals replaced with the clip-ins. I went up the next day, and the bike was once again a cycling bike. I got a pair of SIDI shoes and had clip-in pedals put on. As I waited for little Chris to put on the clip-ins, one of the summer helpers, Beau, asked if I had done the century ride with regular pedals. When I replied that I had, he asked if I were nuts and proceeded to explain the benefit of the clip-in to me. First, your feet will not slip off;, second, and most importantly, is clip-ins allow the rider to push and pull instead of just push, which allows for long distance, better results, and less tired legs, calves, and feet. I told him my feet were killing me and he said, "My point exactly; these will allow you not to push down so hard, your feet are locked in, and you can enjoy more comfort in the lengthy ride."

Once again, I had no clue-but the summer help was right in the thick of things, as if he had worked there for thirty years He was a college kid, yet his communication skills were off the charts. He chuckled a few times, but he knew that his engaging me would allow me to grow, and allow him to grow as well-he guided me onto something so new, as if he had done it a million times One thing he emphasized was to practice unclipping ten times on each foot. He suggested using my mailbox post to stabilize myself and to rehearse on the sidewalk or close to the curb; it would be odd, but he stated the more I practiced, the easier it would be. This youthful kid, a summer assistant, just gave me the time, gave me the knowledge I desired, and helped the customer to perfection-he gets it. He is all IN.

The owner of this shop is a huge cheerleader-his people skills are off the charts, and I can spot that every single time I am there. He is a busy man, like all owners, CEO's, and branch managers, but the glow in his eyes is one for the people. He has a heart for people, I would say, a passion and love for customers and his staff. He is a quiet man, reserved, not a hyperactive or overbearing type, a down-to-earth, laid-back individual who cheers his staff on as a team. He is reputable at what he does, for he has completeness and that spreads like wildfire among the shop He talks with everyone, and talks with intelligence, with a warm soothing voice, and speaks from the heart. He tells the truth, he is up front and brutally honest with me and, I am sure, others. He communicates both verbally and though his actions. He possesses integrity and responsibility, has an excellent work ethic and a humble spirit about him. The shop radiates these concepts of communication, and this shop is as small as an airplane lavatory compared to the massive sporting goods stores. It is not mammoth, it is teeny, -but customers get what they come for, SERVICE-and the shop delivers a blow every time.

# CHAPTER 10 PASSION

"Whatever you are, be a good one."-Abraham Lincoln

The last paragraph nailed the atmosphere of the shop; its ability to display passion for the job, as in so many other bicycle shops across the land, this is why customers continue to revisit. Customers are seeking out passion; they are pursuing the love of the game. People are always taken aback to find staff who nurture their occupation, who demonstrate that notion, and who do it 365 days a year. Why is it that when I go up to the hardware store or the grocery store I see people with passion all the time? Then on the flip side when I visit a store I see people who are just clocking in ready to head home at any given moment. I personally feel that the leader of the facility is the one who sets the tone. I have been around phony people, people who are out to impress everyone, yet while working with the staff they have no clue as to how to lead, so they use intimidation to get their way. This is not leadership, this is being a boss. I read a passage which referred to this as saluting the flag, then kicking the dog syndrome. Out front they are the leader-supposedly leading the way, barking orders, demanding this, saying yes to their boss-then behind closed doors they are kicking everyone down the hallway. This is not leadership at all; this is how cowards lead an organization. So as you walk the stores, take note of a person who is lacking some passion. Wonder if they are the problem, or are they, perhaps, being lead the incorrect way.

Passion for one's job can be the biggest and sweetest payoff while working. At the bicycle shop, I had the impression that all the employees felt a true sense of ownership and believed that they had a stake in the success of the company. . The atmosphere is so laid-back, the store is so spotless, the products are perfectly displayed, and the counters are always sparkling and free of excess debris. Once when I was there getting a tire fixed, I saw one employee cleaning the bathroom-now that is passion. Most places have a cleaning service, but not this one, as far as I could tell. They did it themselves, and that is ownership on display. Not all customers see that, I am sure, but I always seemed to be looking out for those little extras that the general public overlooks. I respect an organization that encompasses all employees, I admire a system that gets the owner and their fellow employees excited to clean the bathroom-if they can get animated about cleaning bathrooms, then they will be thrilled and devoted about filling the needs of customers. They will distribute that work environment with other employees and that will spread like wild-fire-all for one and one for all.

I had been hitting the roads now for a few weeks, and not once did I fall over trying to get out of the clips; I was a pro because of Beau's support. Well, that is how I thought. One day I had been out on a seventy mile jaunt getting ready to cross over a chaotic street, when I went to unclip and I could not get out. There were no cars approaching at the time, and I just panicked and fell over at the stop sign. Of course, when I looked up and was still clipped in, about fifteen cars went by, the drivers all staring at me. I biked the last two miles without clipping in and, sure enough, I got home and I broke the clip and the screws were all loose. I took the shoes up to the store and told Tim, the owner, I had broken my clips and fallen over. With a gracious heart he asked if I was okay and, of course, I told him I was. He looked at the shoes and said the screws had worked free and I was powerless to unclip. He said to go on back and they'd hook me up, and with that the little girl, Jama took over. She got the new clips and proceeded to inform me about why it is so important to tighten the screws. She put the new ones on, oiled the holes and screws, and adjusted the clips to fit my shoes-$40 well spent, and again the passion that loomed in the air was so contagious-everyone was passionate all the time.

A huge term that is used in the bicycle community and in bicycle shops across the land is BICYCLE FITTING. According to the shop's website, bicycling is most comfortable and efficient when your bike is adjusted to fit your body correctly. Okay, that makes sense to me, however, how many people honestly know that the bike has to fit properly? When I mean fit, I mean fit-not just the notion of being able to ride to grandma's house. I mean getting out there and tackling the roads and feeling comfortable at the end of the ride. I would honestly say that the majority of non-riders would say just hop on a bike and go for it. I know when I was younger and I got a ten speed, my dad and I chose it after the employee looked at me and guessed what size I needed; out the door we went. Times have changed, equipment has changed, and the passion for the sport has drastically changed over the years. Today, through technology of such equipment as Fitmaster, Computrainer, LeMond Fitness and Fitkit, as well as high-tech fitting tools and equipment, stores across the land can now fit the customer to the exact specifications his body requires.

My neighborhood shop does these fittings all the time; one thing that stands out is that if you purchase a complete road bike, cyclo-cross, or triathlon bike you get a free comprehensive lifetime bicycle fitting, valued at $250-$300. Now that is passion for the game. I don't know if other shops or stores do this, but if they do, that is awe-inspiring. What I do know is this: it isn't cheap to do a fitting on a bicycle. Time, effort, and planning are involved in this bicycle fitting, and a store employee is tied up for a minimum of two hours. That is two hours off the floor, two hours not answering the phone, two hours not seeing customers-but it is two hours that are the most crucial to any rider. The appropriate fitting of the bicycle and they are furnishing it for FREE if you purchase a new bike. WOW!!!!! Free, who doesn't love FREE? I can tell you this, the store does. They love it and the customer loves it just as much. The most vital task is being taken out of the equation because the owner has passion for his customers and it shines through. Free, nothing is for free. Someone still has to get paid for their services, and that is the store-their passion to drive home the love of cycling is how I see this service being provided.

"Our comprehensive lifetime bicycle fitting takes two hours, and it is done by appointment only. It takes place in our well-equipped fitting area. We'll spend the first half hour or so talking about your past, present, and future experience in cycling. We want to know why you ride your bike, what your goals are, and what you want to achieve with the fitting. We'll discuss what you like and dislike about your current bike and other bikes you may have owned. We'll also talk about pre-existing conditions and how they may affect your fit. After talking in depth with you, we'll take some simple body measurements and lots of measurements of your bicycle. We'll then have you warm up, and we'll begin making changes to your bike. There are basic principles and guidelines at work, and our fitters are more than happy to explain what they're doing and why. We'll also keep extremely detailed measurements and notes on file for future reference." (23)

That is directly from their website-that is what they will do for the customer after they purchase a new bike and this can also be completed for a fee if you bring in your own bike. What catches my eye is the one-on-one time with the customer, which is of no cost to the consumer. The fee is waived upon the purchase of the bike, which enables the shop to get to know the customer and that is passion. The store will eat the cost, but will gain the confidence of the buyer. Okay, now if you buy a bicycle at a supermarket or warehouse, do you get a FREE fitting? The answer is NO. The bicycle shop bestows upon you a FREE fitting and that is devotion to a customer.

One of the bicycles the shop carries is named Moots-in the bicycle's brochure (24) it states the corporation has one thing that will never change, and that is their passion and commitment for building the finest riding bikes possible. For three decades, Moots has been building high-performance bicycle frames. What started off in the back of a small shop in Steamboat Springs, Colorado, has now turned into a major player. . They create Titanium bikes; over the years, they have developed and the technology has sky- rocketed, but according to them, they still have a craze for staying connected to what made them successful. Dogs still roam the factory and lunchtime rides are still the norm. The name has matured, but the mania of the sport still remains steady as it did thirty years ago. Hard work and passion has enabled them to stick to their core values of making a supreme product and keeping the theme alive and well. WOW! Just a start-up industry thirty years ago can today be found far and wide; now that is passion.

While getting up and at them is a true testament to doing the job right, it is also the means to saying you are a Monday person ready to face the week's tasks, not the Friday person; each day waiting and waiting for Friday to approach. Each day telling your co-workers I can't wait for Friday, you are the Monday person each day seeing what needs to be completed, and then doing it again Tuesday, Wednesday, Thursday and Friday. You go home at the end of the work day, knowing you tackled the day head-on and achieved your daily goal, you are fulfilled and it shows. That is a sign of passion, a sign of you are all IN.

One person whom I saw exhibit zest in the workforce is a gentleman by the name of Walter Gill. Walter works at Home Depot in Cordele, Georgia right off of Interstate 75. The image below is of Walter holding up my broken cycling shoes. It was 7 p.m. and we were on US 41 heading south. I banged into a railroad track pretty firm, then I smacked another, and another. Upon crossing all three, I went to unclip my right shoe, and I could not get it out-I panicked and I had to find a telephone pole to keep me upright so I would not just fall over like I did on my first week of using clip-ins. I could not unclip at all-I called to Scott and he turned around and proceeded to aid me getting out. Sure enough, all but one screw was missing-therefore I could not get out. It was pretty late, and by the time we got the bike loaded in the Jeep it was 8 p.m. No cycling shop would be open, so we hit up the car parts shop, but they had no equipment whatsoever to help. The young men helping us suggested we go to Home Depot and see a man by the name of Walter, he is the finest. He told us to walk in and holler WALTER-he is an extraordinary man, one who can pull tricks out of a hat at any given moment-Walter will come through for you.

Scott and I walked in around 8:30 p.m. and yelled WALTER-then we heard aisle after aisle Walter, Walter, Walter, and then this big man came out of an aisle and introduced himself as Walter. He asked how he could lend a hand, so I told him we were cycling to Florida for charity and my cycling shoes broke. I needed screws and washers to reattach them. He told us to get the shoes and meet him in aisle seven. We met him in the screw and washer section; he had a screwdriver and began

his magic. He took the three screws out of the good shoe,-walked to aisles five and six and came back and started to manufacture a brand new clip. He went up and down the aisle grabbing this and grabbing that-he had crimpers, washers, screws, hack saw, super glue and a few other items-the only thing he did not have were scrubs, a mask and surgical gloves. He went to work and by 9 p.m., the broken shoe was back together. His passion for his job was shining through, he was a master at his job, (a shoe repairman beyond his years). We asked him if he had ever done that before; his answer was no, but that did not matter to him. He told us he'd built a robot with an eleven-year old last weekend from scratch, and he had never done that either. Walter was doing what Walter was good at-connecting with people, being himself, being a man of true spirit and a worker who exemplifies passion and commitment to customer service. In one week, he built a robot and built cycling shoes-here he is at Home Depot, a place for homes-yet, Walter was committed to whomever walked in, he was committed to helping others, committed to helping anyone at any time get the job done-that is passion. Walter is one person in a tiny town-but the same thing goes on all over the US and all over the world. People with passion are why businesses are successful, why customers come back, why doors are always open. To all the Walters in the world, I tip my cap.

# CHAPTER 11 PERSEVERANCE

"There will be a lot of complaining that today was too hard, but the winners never complain."-Phil Liggett, Tour De France commentator

If I told you a bicycle company was created over a pickle shop would you believe me? If I told you that company today is world renowned, would you believe me? That company is Cannondale, and in 1971 they did get their birth above a crowded loft in a pickle factory. Over the years they have grown, not only in cycling but also in apparel and accessory lines while still earning a strong reputation for quality and innovation. Cannondale created the first touring bike in 1983, the first road racing and mountain bikes in 1984. In 1997, Cannondale was the first bicycle manufacturer to introduce an oversized aluminum frame at the biggest event, the Tour de France. Cannondale was the role model for the mountain bike boom in the 1980s. According to the National Bicycle Dealers Association, mountain bike sales accounted for 60% of bicycles sold through that period and Cannondale was right there in the thick of things. In 2011, according to the NBDA, 24% of sales were road bikes, 23% were mountain bikes and 20% were hybrid/cycles. Okay, here is the kicker: Cannondale manufactures all three top sellers. They are not just a one man band; they shine in all three categories.

Cannondale has four categories of outstanding equipment they provide their customers: mountain, road, recreation and specification. Under those four categories, they have twelve sub-categories, including over mountain, cross-country full suspension, cross-country hardtails, trail hardtails, elite road, performance road, triathlon/time trial, cyclocross, urban, recreation, specifications, and geometry. Okay, I am not a math whiz, nor am I a super genius-but when you add those up, I must say that is pretty impressive. To be founded in a pickle loft, and today being able to manufacture that many types of bikes I have to tip my hat and say way to go. Perseverance paid off for this company, I must say-to be a leader in any category does not come easy. But to have a stronghold in all three, now that is impressive. I can only imagine the words among the founding members back in the day-you work where? You are doing what? That is crazy, no one will buy that-no one will use that. I am almost positive when I say perseverance through the difficult times and the bumps in the road paid off. In March of 2012, the SuperSix EVO was named the "best bike in the world" by Tour Magazine in Germany. This road bike was built on a perfect blend of all the key factors of performance-weight, stiffness, strength, compliance, handling and aerodynamics, according to Cannondale. (25)

Now, accomplishments just do not come overnight-they are not just created in a dream and, poof, appear on the shelves the next day. Trial and error comes with the territory. Cannondale is competing all the time; they are at the drawing board at Wednesday night crits for those racing in the tour or Megavalanche, to those at the stoplight on the morning commute. We listen, we tweak, we test and we ride some more-as noted in the 2013 Cannondale bicycle brochure.

It was now August 29th and I just completed a 76 mile ride, for a total of 826 miles of training under my belt. My weight was down to 239 pounds and I even shaved my legs, for wind resistance, I thought. I told the shop what I had done, and they asked, "Why?" I said, "Wind resistance," and of course they all laughed, giggled and felt bad for me. They told me I had to go twenty-five miles per hour in order to benefit from shaving my legs. They said the reason riders shave their legs is that it is easier to clean wounds after a wreck. All this time I thought I was going fast because I was hairless, but it made total sense to me, for I averaged only seventeen miles an hour on a century ride.

While I was at the shop, Big Chris was thinking outside of the box. He declared that I had better start doing a few gigantic rides back to back. He said I needed my body to adjust to the rigorous agenda that I would take on in a few weeks. So I took him up on his leadership, and on September 12th I did an eighty-six mile loop, then on September 13th I did another 100 miles or a second century ride. My butt, arms, and legs felt extraordinary. I could not believe I just did 186 miles in two days. Then Little Chris said you need to get a feel for what the roads are like when you have never seen them before. Big Chris jumped right in and said, "Ride your bike to Cincinnati, see your mom and dad, and get a notable ride in for preparation."

After getting the two day jaunt behind me, I phoned the friend who had donated the bicycle for the cause and told him about my accomplishments. Needless to say, he was very ecstatic about the journey, but he asked if Scott and I were still planning on sharing the bike, and of course, I said yes. He continued to explain that raising the seat and adjusting this and that will be very time consuming. He would like to donate another bike for me and have Scott use the red one. With that, my friend would share another bike with us; this one was a Roark, a very sleek bike made out of all titanium, and it weighed almost nothing. This was a huge favor, perfect timing, to say the least. Big HEART my buddy has.

I took their suggestion, and on October 3rd left Indianapolis and cycled through four little towns, up and down hills, and into Cincinnati city limits. I did not make it into downtown Cincy, but I did get to experience what it was going to be like in three weeks. I was chased by two dogs, one gas station gave me a hard time when I brought the bike inside for a bathroom break, and I got lost twice and had to get back on track. It took me two hours to get out of Indianapolis because of traffic, stop signs, and red lights. Once I got outside of the major city, I was flying. I learned to appreciate good drivers, and learned to appreciate excellent customer service. I learned to persevere through the regimen, for I was not going to give up-I made it this far and Cincinnati was just another milestone to cross off. I left at 7 a.m. and arrived in Cincy at 5:30p.m.-1309 miles of training under my belt, with the help of the pros at the bicycle shop.

If you want to be the best in the business, you have to learn to persevere. There is no stronger term in the business thesaurus than that word, in good times and in bad times. To persevere in any business, one must be ready and able to commit one's self to understanding the current market and the current trends. The current trend is this-bicycle lanes are growing, as I noted earlier, all over the United States; they are being fought for in communities, cities and states everywhere. That is the current trend. On your way to church, school, or work, take a look around and see the bike lanes; some are marked in green or light red, and some are striped. Cycling is being brought to the forefront in our daily lives for the sake of the environment and as a great means to get our daily exercise. That is the current trend. Now, as a store owner, we have to understand that not every single person coming in is going to buy a $5,000 or $10,000 bike. But, what can materialize is we can capture them, mold them, share with them our passion and lust for the sport so that when they are ready to drop a few big bucks we have them already in our grips. We have them in our grasp, because the customer knows us, they believe in us, they share a common thread of empathy with us, as well as us to them. A one and done is far from the truth-it may be for the time being, but why do customers keep coming back? Because customers rely on our expertise on the subject they need or want, and we have had to persevere with grace in order to maintain our doors open. We are not just in our fifth or sixth year of being open-we are in our eighth, tenth, twentieth, or fiftieth year because we persevered. This perseverance is a reflection of how much we care about customer service and we will see to it that customers come first, sales second-for the sale is never done.

Shoes-so simple, yet in the cycling world, it can be a tough choice. There are quite a few types of shoes to choose from ranging from Shimano, Mavic, Sidi, Giro, and Pearl Izumi. One shoe that I used on the trip is Sidi; to be honest, I did not have a clue as to why I was using those. It was a shoe, and it clipped into the pedals and that was good enough for me. I didn't really know or understand the different types, weights, and materials of the shoes; I just thought they were all the same. As a matter of fact, when I went to buy my first shoe for the road bike, I was looking at mountain bike shoes and the salesman had to tell me I was looking at the wrong types; just shows you how green I was to the sport.

Perseverance is an excellent term to describe not only my experience riding the bicycle, but what I learned through writing this book, training, and of course the 1000 mile trek: we all have to fight to gain what we want. We can never give up, we have to fight through the rain, sun, setbacks, economy, changes, and we have to adapt and conform to our surroundings or we can be eaten alive. As I was training for the adventure, the summer months in Indiana were excruciating, with temperatures often exceeding 100 degrees. The drought was horrible and the weather conditions just seemed to get worse the more acquainted I became with riding the bicycle. Here I was getting ready to ride to Florida, and the heat (no pun intended) was just off the charts. I had to find a way to succeed on this mission, so I started riding the bicycle first thing in the morning, or really late in the evening. I had to adjust my sails-I was not going to sit back and wait for cooler days. I had my compass set on heading south, so I knew I had to adjust my training and, in due time, cooler weather would arrive. I just wished it would have been sooner, but beggars cannot be choosers. I had to persevere through it, it was only temporary, and I knew if I could dig deep good things would be on the horizon.

A company of any type has got to fight, claw and scrap in the early stages of growth. It is only a vision or concept or even a prototype, but if you stick with it, if you stay the course, all GREAT dreams will come to a head, and success will find its way to you. Sidi, the maker of the shoes I wore, exemplifies that concept. The founder of Sidi is Dino Signori, he has been a part of the cycling community since he was fifteen years old, when he began racing bicycles. He began producing footwear in 1960 in Italy, where he assembled the mountain sports footwear. In 1970, he grew his business into making cycling footwear for bicycles and motorcycles, then in 1973, Sidi produced and designed the titanium cycling shoe. For years, cyclists had to nail cleats into cycling shoes. But with a vision, Mr. Signori persevered and came up with a shoe that would help ease the concept of the sport. His design of the titanium shoe revolutionized cleat attachment with the use of adjustable screws; cyclists could now fit their shoes into the right position increasing power and decreasing injury. Then in 1985, Sidi produced the first ever mountain bike cycling shoe with lugged rubber soles.

Sidi has over fifty years of designing top quality footwear-they also designed the shoe with a nylon sole to give stiffness, used Velcro closure systems, and invented the first micro-adjust buckle in the cycling industry. While researching the back ground of Sidi, I found them to be a company that is adjusting to the growth of the sport-they are looking beyond today, they are looking towards the future. According to Sidi, in 2011 they were designing a shoe that would fit the entry level rider's pocket book; the shoe is called the Nevada, and it is a stiff, weightless shoe that is priced right. (26)

I live here in Indiana, and the Sidi shoe was invented in Italy. I am not flying back and forth to pick up shoes, nor am I having them shipped over First Class, just so I can say I use them. I am simply stating what would have happened to the cycling shoe had Mr. Signori not spread his vision among fellow cyclists? Would the technology of today's cycling shoe be the same as we know it? Or would there have been another person who would have persevered and grew his/her concept? He did not give up; through trial and error, he rose to the occasion and came out a champion on the other side. It took years and years of preparation, years of research, years of marketing, years of passion, and years of stick-to-it-ivity, as Walt Disney would say, to create a masterpiece.

This is why Ben and Jerry's Ice Cream did so well, this why the Big Wheel did so well, this is why Legos are still played with by my daughter and her friends, why Lincoln Logs are still being sold, why Pac Man is still played, why Slip and Slides are still used in backyards across the country. The idea is creative, the concept is revolutionary-but it is the sheer guts to run to the front of the line and say, I am sticking with this and I will make this happen.

mention Walt Disney quite a few times in this book-I feel he is a man of pure heart, a man who never gave up on his dream, and a man who we think of when we hear the word persevere. He is a man who never gave up hope, never folded his cards, and never stopped imagining what he could do next. The bicycle shop next to my house is as small as the bathrooms at Walt Disney World, but walking in you feel right at home. You sense being accepted, you feel special and you feel good about entering. I enjoy Walt Disney World a great deal, I look for all the little hidden Mickeys, I look for all the little human touches, I feel the zest from the employees, and I feel good about myself when I leave. I feel the equivalent at the bicycle shop-but all grand things had to appear at a price, THE PRICE OF PERSEVERING.

# CHAPTER 12 BOND

"The single most important thing to remember about any enterprise is that there are no rules inside its walls. The result of a business is a satisfied customer."-Peter Drucker

As a father of an eight-year-old daughter who is into gymnastics, horseback riding, and wrestling with her dad, I have, over the years, attached quite a few Band-Aids. When I was a kid, my parents did the identical step, as well as millions of other parents across the country. There was the accident, there was the little cut, and of course, there was the blood. To state they were critical is a far cry, but to the little child it is a huge crisis. We have to connect with them, we have to understand it is a big deal; we forge a promise that everything is going to be okay. The Band-Aid commercial, and I can still recall the tune, was the best and still is to this day. It goes like this-I am stuck on Band-Aid brand 'cause Band-Aid's stick on me, I am stuck on Band-Aid brand cause germs don't stick on me, cause they hold on tight no matter what on fingers, toes and knees, I am stuck on Band-Aid brand 'cause Band-Aids stick on me. Two things stand out in this ad -one, the band aids did stick; and two, it lead to comfort and resulted in reassurance that everything was going to be all right immediately. It still works to this day and it will work in the future. Something as simple as applying a Band-Aid to a wound takes all the bad stuff out of the mind of a child. Band-Aids are just that: they aid in recovery, they assist in healing, and they bond and forge a connection from parent to child that all is going to be fine, and we will be happier after we bond this to your finger, toe or elbow. At the beginning, my child, like so many others, thinks everything is terrible, then after applying the Band-Aid, she thinks everything is in good health. The Band-Aid brings everything to conclusion. Once it is applied, my daughter is good to go.

    Okay; that is just splendid, but what does a Band-Aid have to do with a bicycle shop? The answer is EVERYTHING. I have created a bond with my child, my wife has created a bond with our child, and together as a team we both have created a bond with our child. Maggie knows that if she gets hurt, needs help with her homework, or needs to just talk, we are there for her. The Band-Aid is just the gadget, the conviction she has in us to help her is the connection we have. The same goes for the bicycle shop-sure they sell bicycles, but that is not why I keep going there. I go there because I feel the bond they bestow upon me, as well as the thousands of other customers that stroll in their door. I have been up there for no other reason except just to meander in and say hello. I have been up there just to feel positive that I made the correct decision to ride my bicycle a thousand miles-they are providing me with a sense of protection. They don't even realize what they are providing me-it just comes natural, and that is the bond in business. That is the bond in customer service which fuses our relationship together as one.

    It was October 16th, the last day of training, and I got in thirteen miles around the neighborhood to close up with 1400 miles of training. So the next day, I headed up to the bicycle shop to get all the gear I needed for the expedition -tubes, pump, reflective lights, back flashing light, Hammer Gels, ProBars, extra tires, multi-tool, and an array of other items. The total bill was over $250. But the one characteristic that stood out that day was the bond the staff had with me. They kept telling me, "You will make it," "Call us if you have any questions," "Tell us all about it when you get back," "Have fun first, and get there safely." Earlier in the book, I talked of a man with a beard. I did not interface with

Brad (Einstein) very much, but this day I did. He walked up to me and asked, "Can you change a tire and a tube?" I said, "No." He said, "Now is the time." With that, Brad, the Einstein of the mechanics bay, taught me how to change a tube and how to change a tire with the multi-tool. We did it not once, but three times. He gave me his cell number and said, "Please, please, call me if you have any problems." Then he said, "YouTube is another great way to see it on the road if you forget."

Another sale went sour, because the shop was watching out for me, and not for their profit. I knew it was going to be cold when we left-I am not a weatherman, but I could see it was going to be chilly in the early morning and late in the evening. I informed the shop I needed to purchase a jumpsuit for the ride; once again they all chuckled at me, for they knew exactly what I needed. All of them sent me over to the clothing rack for sleeves and leggings. They told me to wear my normal biking gear and put the sleeves on my arms and the leggings on my legs. I would have layers, and when I became hot, I could take them off, and still have my cycling outfit on. WOW!!!!-they understood my wallet, they understood sound advice, and they understood quality. They delivered it right there and then. The shop could have sold me a $300 suit, but they sold me $40 sleeves and $45 leggings-which I wore every single day. $215 less profit, but this is what once again sold me on why I shop there.

The shop's staff was not sending out a newbie into the wilderness, they were sending a first-rate cyclist out into the real world with the utmost confidence. I was about to depart in three days, and I had a bond with a shop that was out of this world. ALL of them shook my hand, little Jama even gave me a hug, and they all said, "Go get 'em." One person, Joel, whom I had not interacted with once over last 140 days, sold me all the accessories I needed, and we talked for a half hour about the safety of my journey. With that I knew my voyage was created on a bond-created on friendship that was forged on day one. I never in my wildest dreams thought I could ride a bike to Florida, and I was seventy-two hours away from that start. I felt so attached to the shop, I felt so safe and sound knowing that I made the right decision to see the pros.

In the book The Starbucks Experience, author Joseph A. Michelli talks about Five Principles for Turning Ordinary into Extraordinary. In the book, he gives five bullet points as to what makes Starbucks successful-number five is Leave your Mark. He states-

"Once your company moves from a business that sells a product, to a business that makes a difference, it will naturally attract more business, entice more talented candidates to join the team, foster higher employee morale, enjoy boosted productivity, and eventually realize higher profits." (27)

Make a difference. WOW, now that is how I see the bicycle shop. This bicycle shop, just like all the bicycle shops in the United States and in the world, is striving to connect with customers. On day one, this shop connected and forged a bond. This is going to sound crazy, but I had this experience once before in the dental field. Her name was Doctor Barbara A. Cain. I was discharged honorably form the Navy back in 1996, and, after settling down back in my home town of Anderson Township, a little community east of Cincinnati out in the suburbs, I had to locate a dentist. Sure enough my girlfriend, now my wife, told me about her dentist and how wonderful she was; she was friendly, she made you feel welcomed and she made you feel at ease. I picked up the phone and lined up the appointment, and she delivered exactly what my wife said. For four years, until moving to Indianapolis, she was my dentist. For four years, she was the best in the field to me. She had a relaxed atmosphere, she provided the best dental care, and she had the nicest assistant who reflected Dr. Cain's values and customer service standards. I looked forward to every single visit-some were not as pleasant as others, which was my fault, but she forged a bond with me, she connected with me and she made me feel comfortable going to that practice. Why? Like Michelli stated in his book, she left her mark on me, she made a difference on my teeth, and delivered a knockout punch on what a relaxed atmosphere means. Dr. Cain, DDS was my dentist because someone else had a similar experience and wanted all to know about her practice, because she delivered what the customer sought after. If we move back to Cincinnati, she would be my dentist.

On August 15, 2012 the Los Angeles Times wrote an article about Home Depot and Lowe's customer service push. (28) In that article, Dalina Castellanos writes:

The big home improvement companies have been busy directing store clerks to spend more time with customers, improving the information and advice they offer in online catalogs, installing Wi-Fi computer service in stores and improving do-it-yourself instructions.

She also states that. In 2009, Home Depot introduced a plan aimed at devoting 60% of an associate's time to helping customers rather than the previous focus on stocking shelves and cleaning the stores. In 2012, just before the busy spring season, every employee was retrained under the Customers First initiative. Home Depot has 1,976 stores nationwide. Do you know how many employees would have to get trained? A ton, but Home Depot understands that customer service needs to be revisited time after time. It can't all be about profit, so 60% is about customer service. WOW!!!!! If Home Depot understands it, who else can grasp it? Everyone, far and wide. We can learn a lot from a well-respected company. However, Ace Hardware has understood that concept for years, ranking highest in customer service for the last six years in an annual survey conducted by J.D. Power and Associates.

Why do I enjoy the bicycle shop? Because the bicycle shop put me before the sale. They positioned my needs before their needs. The bond I felt on day one is the same way I felt on day 150. I felt a promise, I felt a pledge, I felt security, and I felt a warranty was in place by word of mouth and not a piece of paper. I felt the notion of we have your back, we are looking out for you, we understand you, and most of all I felt the nexus of we were looking out for each other. The bond, the thread that held us together was the reason our link never broke-it is a paste, super glue, a binding that is the core of the store's values and the store's mission.

Another angle to bond with the times is looking at cool ways of connecting with customers; travel.spotcoolstuff.com (29) has a section on the cool bicycle shops. According to them, the best bicycle shops do more than fix and sell bicycles, they fill you with a sort of enthusiastic energy that makes you want to get out there and pedal. One shop in Altlandsberg, Germany has 120 bicycles attached to the exterior of the building, and on weekends Berliners will ride twenty kilometers to visit and hang out in the garden or playground out front. Another angle to bond with customers is bicycle shops doubling as a coffee shop-such as Sedona Bike & Bean, Angry Catfish Bicycle and The Ride Studio café. Another one is called the Old Spokes Home in Burlington, Vermont. There they specialize in rehabbing old bicycles which come with a lifetime guarantee, and the shop is an old-fashioned wooden store with an on-site bicycle museum.  Dutch Bike Company in Seattle serves coffee and offers chocolate cookies while you wait on your bike or browse the store.  Last one that stood out was Pave in Barcelona-there you can buy bikes, read books and magazines in their library, enjoy the café, watch a race on an array of TVs, or even get cleaned up in the showers they offer.

    A lot has changed over the years, and many more amenities other than bicycle paraphernalia are offered. But one thing that has not changed in the industry is that no matter what extras you offer your customers, no matter what reels them in-sale, holiday special, anniversary price- you still have to bond with the customer and offer them quality service. Coffee, wine, beer, showers, TVs, library, Wi-Fi-all of those are great, but you still have got to make a bond and fuse with the customer. Customers are not stupid, they are looking for more than fireworks; they are looking for more than 15% off, 20% off, half priced items or even buy one get one free.  They return because they like YOU- that is it. They like the encounter they had, the conversation they had, the attention they were provided which then provides them a sense of warmth and security in knowing they made the correct decision to stay with your store for future purchases-they go back to the best, because you gave them the best.

# CHAPTER 13 FLORIDA, HERE I COME

"If you build a great experience, customers tell each other about that. Word of mouth is very powerful."-Jeff Bezos, Amazon.com

The frequent customer, the regular customer, any way you put it, is of great value. El Rodeo restaurant right behind my house serves the best Mexican food in town, in my opinion. I do not eat Mexican food all the time, but when I do, I go to El Rodeo. The reason they win me over is the personal touch. The minute I walk in, they shake hands with me, they ask how I am doing, ask how my wife is, and ask my little girl how she is doing. Then, right off the bat, they know I would like a diet coke, my wife water, and my daughter pink lemonade. They proceed to take the order with acute accuracy, deliver a quality product, and deliver harmony between the restaurant and my family, they understand it. That is why I am a customer for life. The food is good, the atmosphere is good, but the perpetual personal touch is the value I enjoy the most.

Andy Ording is the founder of Zipp wheels. In an article in Road Bike Action Magazine, Andy is asked, of all the different product categories, what is it about wheels that propel Zipp forward? Andy- "We built a brand and the company on the back of our wheels and the races won on them-seeing our wheels in the races like the Ironman and the Tour de France gives us a sense of pride that fuels that energy- The short-lived satisfaction of a race victory only serves to propel us to imagine how much faster the wheels can be". (30)

Andy understands it, for the example is in his reply-short-lived. He celebrates with his customers on victories and accomplishments, but Zipp does not stop delivering quality. They are propelling forward, they are looking beyond today, and they see more return, more investment, more kinship and partnerships in the future to forge with customers and clients. Stores stockpile these wheels, the hardware, and the components because Zipp delivers growth to their customers, to the riders, to the racers, to the Ironman, to the Tour de France. Customers return because Zipp continues to make quality products which, in turn, creates an off the charts experience for the rider. The customers (riders, store owners) come back for more and come back with an endless, ageless and everlasting bond that makes them a customer for life.

The bicycle shop is exactly that notion-they high five the sale, the fitting, the advice they give a veteran or a newbie, then they press on. They don't stop in their tracks and say look at me. The shop has more customers on the horizon. They need to celebrate the day's victories and end on a positive note, then start the whole process over the next day. We all know how our favorite movies begin and end, but to a business, each day starts a new sequel. Each day brings on new scenes, characters and scenery, but the main theme of the movie must remain the same: CUSTOMERS FIRST.

Recipients, consumers, prospects, patrons, clients, customers all have a choice to make in their buying habits, but why is it that people continue to return and return again? The Washington Post ran an article called "How to Breed Innovation Inside a Small Business." In this insightful read, the writer, Drew Marshall, nails it with his delivery. He states, "Most (businesses) have close relationships with their customers, and because of the personal connections they have forged, those customers tend to have a vested, emotional interest in the enterprise's success. Never underestimate the power of emotion-and take advantage of it to drive innovation." (31)

October 20, 2012, was a morning I will never forget (my dad's birthday). Up and at 'em at 5 a.m., I loaded up my suitcase, supplies,

## CHAPTER 13 FLORIDA, HERE I COME

and Scott's equipment. John and Kathy, my neighbors across the street, and Steve, my next door neighbor, came out and wished us good luck. I kissed my wife and little girl goodbye and told them I loved them very much. We drove up to the bicycle shop and started our journey south at 7 a.m.-we had to start from the shop, they got us this far, why not start there? Our first stop was in Louisville, Kentucky-we had to make it there by sundown and, sure enough, 13.5 hours later we made it. Crossing the river at 8:30 p.m.-we made it. Stop one in the books.

Being inventive, being creative is what drives business. We see a whole slew of choices all the time, just open Sunday's paper and look at all the marketing, coupons, ads trying to drive the consumer to their establishment. All of those help-but what separates the good from the great is the stronghold of obtaining a customer for life. My neighborhood bicycle shop has done that with me. Day one could have gone sour, but because of honesty, they won me over. My bicycle shop is no different than the nationwide chain of auto parts, the nationwide chain of department stores, the nationwide chain of barber shops and restaurants. What separates the good from the great is the first initial encounter between the store and the customer. We did not invent HELLO-it has been around for years; yet, that simple, little, kind word hits home to so many people.

Newspapers and TV claim that society is in a big rush, we are in a huge hurry to get things done and move on. We want instant gratification. We do not have time to dillydally around; when we want something, we want it now. If you want a bicycle you can get one now, but if you want a quality product that comes with a quality encounter, one that will give you more than a bicycle, then go to your local bicycle shop and see what I am talking about. You will not be disappointed at all-the craftsmanship that goes into a bicycle is the same as a great baker or chef.

On October 21st we were up and at 'em at 5 a.m. again. Scott and I took turns riding-we rode 50% thus far, and today we were going to do the same. Our destination was Nashville, Tennessee. Scott was first to go, and we proceeded on US 41 South. Sure enough half way, we traded spots and now I was riding. We made it as close as twenty miles from Nashville, but it was 8:15 at night so we had to call it quits. We had to average 150 miles a day in order for us to make it to Orlando on the

26th. I had never eaten so much in my life-day two in the books-we were running on pure adrenaline. Our bodies felt great, my knee was feeling great, my hands were fine, and my butt was in good shape.

There is more to it than just buying a product or service. The bicycle shop next to my house is engaged with the local community. They have a cycling team which the store supports, they have benefit rides for causes that the store and clients hold dear, and of course they offer evening rides as a team. Two days a week the shop holds rides, sometimes exceeding 200 cyclists, ranging from the beginner to the advanced. The store does not care how fast you can go, or how long you can ride-they just want the customer to be a part of the journey. They offer more than just selling bikes; they are connecting with people, with the community, and are sharing their passion with others. People who may never have stepped foot in the door are happy to be a part of the day's ride. It is innovative and creative to conduct these rides, but the shop just wants to give cyclists and enthusiasts more than they expect because the shop loves cycling.

On October 22nd we were again on the road at 7 am-Scott was riding and our destination was Chattanooga, Tennessee. Hills, Hills and more hills-all the training we put in over the last five months was about to pay off-and sure enough at 8 p.m., we rolled into the city limits. Scott was chased by a dog, and at one point I was going 44 miles per hour downhill, and also going 2 miles per hour up hill. Pretty dangerous if you ask me, but I felt the bicycle shop set me up to succeed at this point-all the preparation and guidance they gave us was really set in stone and it was working out great, better than we had planned.

Why did I go back to the shop after the first day? Here are examples of what others shops offer across the country. Pedal House in Laramie, Wyoming gives out free trail maps, as well as great advice to beginners and supports local racers. Freeze Thaw Cycles in State College, Pennsylvania pride themselves on offering service. Wheel and Sprocket in Hales Corner, Wisconsin supports more than twenty charity rides and sponsors seven race teams. Fat Tire Farm in Portland, Oregon has such great mechanics that sixty other shops have been known to bring their mechanics their difficult suspension fixes. Bicycle Habit in New York City has been a key force in pushing for a more bike-friendly New York since 1978. Above Category in Mill Valley, California has intimate product knowledge which has earned customers who won't shop anywhere else. Sports Garage in Boulder, Colorado has employees who are passionate riders and provide first-class customer service. Fit Werx in Waitsfield, Vermont has a bike-fit magician who has customers riding with less pain and more power.

Here is an actual review of a Charleston Bicycle Co. in Charleston, South Carolina written by Jeff S. (32)

"I live two hours away and drove in on a Saturday morning to purchase and get fitted for a new bike. The team (and yes, there was more than one person who helped me!) was spectacular. When I arrived, my bike was already up on the fitting stand and Mike (who I had spoken to several times on the phone and was outstanding at keeping me up to date on sizes, stock, availability, etc.) was standing there, tools in hand, ready to get me sized. Once we took measurements off my old bike, Mike and the guys got me all set up on my new Cervelo, and turned me loose on the neighborhood roads behind the shop to test out my new bike. While I was getting settled in, Mike was riding alongside to show me around where I would be riding, and take additional looks at my fit from the perspective of riding alongside. I could not have asked for a better overall experience. Seriously, I've travelled all over the place visiting local bike shops and some are great and some are just bad. This one is in the "great" category. They're friendly, knowledgeable, passionate about cycling, and most important, they *help* you. I would go back to them in a heartbeat".

Here is another review of Winter Park Cycles, in Orlando, Florida written by Brian H. (33)

Being a new road cyclist, and someone who is really starting to get into it, I had a slew of questions about cycling from fitting, to nutrition, to bike components and frames. Daryl (as well as the others that were in the store) were extremely patient with me and answered all my questions from the vantage point of experienced and passionate cyclists. I truly felt like they had my personal best interests at heart. Like I said; true professionals.

These customer reviews that I found on Google Reviews are a sign of customers' experiences that are off the charts. Customers do not take the time to place these unless they are truly satisfied with their overall experience, and they want the world to know what happened to them.

Bicycle shop after bicycle shop have these reviews up-reviews are the way customers express their gratitude and convey their feelings toward an excellent or unpleasant outing. YES-there are unpleasant reviews, they are a part of the wide scope, people are not going to get what they came in for, they are going to be let down as they would put it, but in reality timing, the day, the weekend, the hour may have come into play. Going up on Saturday to get a haircut at 11 a.m. is not the best time in the world to get one, nor is getting my car washed at noon on Saturday. Timing is everything-going to look at paint on Saturday at noon is probably not the best solution either, so as a customer take into consideration what day of the week it is, and what time you are going in. If it is a huge purchase, a huge process, don't show up at 5:45 when the store closes at 6. If that happens, I believe the great ones will help out. Keep in mind they have a life outside of work as well as you do, so don't hold a grudge if you feel rushed.

October 23rd-once again up and at 'em, headed from Chattanooga to Atlanta. . At this point, I could make the best waffle in the world at the continental breakfast. I never ate so much in my life-I was burning calories like they were going out of style. It was only 138 miles-but our recoveries from the last previous days were taking a beating. We agreed that the first rider would go the farthest, and the second would be more rested for the next day. Sure enough hills, hills, and more hills during the first part of the day, and after that a little flatter. Still 138 miles seemed like 200 miles-our bodies were starting to feel it. But adrenaline still was thriving-Orlando, we are going to make it.

# CHAPTER 14 I'LL BE BACK

"The purpose of every business and organization is to get and keep customers."-Shep Hyken

A customer for life is the payoff of outstanding performance by a store or service. Customers love a good time and enjoy friendly atmosphere, but in reality they leave being satisfied with their decision to enter your business. Why do people get season tickets to NBA, NFL, NCAA, and MLB? Because they enjoyed it so much, why not all year round. The same goes for convenience stores, salons, shoe stores, and barber shops; customers revisit because they have a high batting average of success and the store delivers a renowned product and service. Customers are not buying the store, they are buying the human touch, they are buying wisdom, they are buying commitment, they are buying friendship-that is why customers are for life. Sure, a variety of products, a sparkling store, and spotless bathrooms get customers back, but customers come back because they want to come back to what they experienced.. They were a part of the squad, part of the assembly, part of the overall scope of the business. They sensed all in from the word go.

October 24th, up again before sunrise-we were headed towards Macon, Georgia. We passed Atlanta Motor Speedway, and zoomed south.

The roads were getting flatter, but our momentum was getting slower. What helped was chocolate milk for recovery and eating the correct meals-spaghetti and lasagna for dinner. We snacked on ProBars and Hammer products, but at this point pure adrenaline was still thriving.

October 25th we left Cordele, Georgia and headed for Gainesville, Florida, still on US 41 south. We had met Walter the night before at Home Depot-my shoes were first class and into Florida we went. Orange trees were popping up all over the place and the University of Florida was right down the street.

This book was written about Nebo Ridge, a bicycle shop next to my house. This shop took me from zero to 2000 miles in 150 days. In 150 days, their wisdom got me to Florida, as well as vision, patience and balance. It was commitment, knowledge and communication that got me on the correct path. It was equipment that enabled me to grow correctly, and it was the bond that was built that made this trip a success. The shop allowed me to persevere with dignity, which was fueled by their passion for delivering quality customer service.

You may have noticed I did not purchase a bicycle from this shop-I did not acquire any fancy equipment for the off season, nor did I carry on with any winter training upon completion. But, what I did seize from this experience is that I am a customer for life, and when the time is right I will buy a top-quality product from them. In the months leading up to my departure for Florida, I spent $1250 in accessories, tune ups, equipment and other amenities. If one hundred customers spent that much money then that equals $125,000, not a bad little payoff without securing a bicycle. This shop is of the highest caliber that delivers unerringly what people are searching for, and it holds bona fide across the United States and the world.

There are around five thousand bicycle shops in the United States, which are five thousand choices customers have. I choose this one because of day one-they reeled me in and caught my attention because they cared enough about my vision on the first day. The first contact, the first handshake, and the first verbal exchange were the deciding factors. Think about it for a second. Why is that you are a customer or a regular at a certain location? We talked about little things, bathrooms, coffee, TVs-but in reality it is the human connection that keeps us going back and back again-if you encompass it, your business will thrive.

## CHAPTER 14 I'LL BE BACK    149

If you don't, bring that feature up and work on it day in and day out.

On October 26, 2012, I rolled into Orlando, Florida and I hit my final destination-I completed my expedition. After arriving safely at the Amway Center and seeing my friend, whom I gave a hug, I phoned my wife and little girl and informed them we made it safely. Then I called up the bicycle shop. My second call was to the shop that made this materialize. I will say it again: my second call was to Nebo Ridge. I passed on a huge thank you and told them how appreciative I was for educating me in a sport I did not have a clue about. Big Chris answered the phone and conveyed a congratulations, and that I was the reason I made it-but in reality it was the two of us that made it a reality-teamwork in motion made this a success, customer service landed me in Orlando.

On October 27th, we were up and at 'em at 6 a.m. and on the road at 7, headed back to Carmel, Indiana. We rolled into our neighborhood a little after 11 p.m. Sixteen hours later our journey was completed and completed safely.

# EPILOGUE

It is awe-inspiring looking back and seeing what can emerge in 150 days, but what is more than awesome is the constructive effect it took on me, my friend Scott, and all the people with whom we interacted and crossed paths along the way. We were able to raise a little over $5,000 on this voyage, divided up among Multiple Myeloma Research Foundation, The Prospect House, International Reading Association, and The American Foundation for Suicide Prevention. Putting people foremost is what the whole trip was about, it is what we strive to do every single day, both in our personal lives and at work. Sometimes, it is hard; but we have to take a step back and really focus on what is important and that is others. There is a great website called I AM SECOND--meaning put others first, ourselves second. I think that sets the tone for customer service as well; work hard, play hard and see each person as a lifelong connection. We have to strive to give customers more than what they are looking for; competition is fierce, and what can set us apart from the rest of the pack is giving a little more, going the extra step, taking that extra initiative and delivering more than what is anticipated.

The bicycle shop--just like others throughout the world-- understands that they are a living, breathing part of the neighborhood. The place where the first bike was purchased, the first group ride commenced, the place where friendships were forged and, of course, where the off-season spinning classes are conducted. But, the social aspect is more than talking; it is being a unit of one with the community--teaching safety, teaching the basics to the advanced. For every customer is different; each has different needs, different wants, different expectations. But, you can never go wrong on listening and delivering. From the five dollar purchase to the twenty-thousand dollar purchase, one never knows what the outcome will be and if the consumer experience is outstanding, they will be back. They will bring their friends and of course they will shout it on the rooftops what an outstanding customer service experience they had.

    As I noted earlier in the book, I did not continue with cycling; however what transpired since then is what customer service and community is all about. My daughter (9 years old) tried cycling with Midwest Devo, which is a U23 cycling development team. Tim, the owner of NeboRidge, called me up after he knew my daughter enjoyed the shop and recommended that she sign up for the team. I took his lead and we headed up to learn more about it. We had committed to summer softball and horse lessons, so the schedule did not work out for us. Because of Tim we now are aware of the group.

    Tim, like so many owners, understands community involvement; he grasps the notion of giving others more than a sale or a brochure. He and his staff give customers their passion of the business; that is the community involvement. Of course, where did we go to get my daughter's cycling equipment? You guessed it, Nebo Ridge. New helmet, new gloves and, of course, a full mountain bike tune-up. We gave them our business, because NeboRidge gives us more than what we want, they are delivering people first, sale second......They repeat those steps over and over and over.....PEOPLE FIRST.

    Before this book went into print, I started a new adventure in my life. I took on a new occupation as Operations Manager with G2 Secure Staff at the Indianapolis Airport. They handle almost every single endeavor when it comes to airport operations. Overseeing security services, parking lot security, hangar protection, sports team charters, skycaps, bag runners, wheelchair agents, lost and found, ramp services, aircraft cleaning, water services, cargo agents, ticket agents, mail services, in-flight services, and many additional responsibilities at nearly fifty airports nationwide. The amount of interaction this position requires is very impressive. As my interview with the General Manager concluded, she asked, "Do you know what business we are in?" Before I could respond, she replied, "The People Business." The next day, I was training with Eric. He said, "Jim, do you know what business we are in?" Before I could react he said, "The People Business." This carried over to my training with, Antwan, Tom, Brandy, Helen, Shalu and the whole staff. It then bleeds over to all who require our services at the airport.

"The people business." What exactly does that mean? Well, in my twenty-five years of being in customer service, it means putting others before your needs. But, that does not just include patrons, it also includes the workforce, the employees.

I hope this book brought you new insight into what it takes to build a customer/business relationship. I hope it makes you think about what it takes to deliver grade A service, and not just the bottom line or dollar. Money runs a business, but people create the business. Deliver more, be honest, resolve all conflict quickly and have FUN. That is the key to customer service. Love what you do so much, that others sense that notion. Customers will give repeat business and tell their friends or even write a book about their experience. The end is never in sight. Like the

CRO, leave the set on REPEAT. Not shuffle, or skip, REPEAT. Day after day, give customers more than they need. Plus it! Legendary coach John Wooden said, "Make each day your masterpiece." I would like to add, why not make each customer your masterpiece?

# EPILOGUE 2 THE RETURN

As I noted earlier in the book I did not buy a bicycle from the shop. It has been nearly two years since my bicycle journey commenced and that friendship and loyalty is as strong today as it was my first day. However in the summer of 2014 my family did go to Nebo Ridge to buy my daughter a new mountain bike for her 10th birthday. What Nebo gave me and my family is a reason to return, a reason to purchase a big item like this for my daughter. My loyalty to the shop/business is off the charts-so myself, my dad, my mom, wife and daughter all headed up to the shop to purchase the bike for her birthday.

Customer loyalty is the biggest pay off for superb customer service, it is the reason business stay open-it is the reason people shop over and over at the same establishment....I am a evangelist for Nebo Ridge and all the staff up there, and that is why we bought the bike from them.

Below is a picture of my daughter and Joel from Nebo-it is a display of customer service that just radiates off the charts. The picture is perfect, it hits the core of putting people first. Here he is talking with my daughter about the new Cannondale, explaining to her(the customer) all the ins and outs of the bike-but I want to take this one step further.

While picking out the bike-Tim the owner was there, he shook my hand and my parents and my wife's hand and extended a hardy wel-

come. The whole staff-Tim, Brad, Brian, Steve, Nate, Jama, Scott, Beau, Tim, Joel, and Charlie all came into play this day-yes, some were not there. But they are/were the reason I am loyal customer because ALL gave me a epic customer experience.

As you can tell from the picture, my daughter's toes only hit the ground. This is because Nebo said buy for the future and not for today. They claimed summer will go by fast, so purchase for the next two summers and with that we bought a women's size bike. Once again they were watching out for our wallet and putting our needs first, another WOW! moment on why they are ranked in the top 100 bike shops in the USA.

The story will never end-I will return over and over as need be, or just to stop by and say hello.

A true loyal customer was formed.

# NOTES

1. Encore Effect—2008, Mark Sanborn, The DoubledDay Publishing Group, Division of Random House, Inc., New York
2. CNN Money. August 9, 2012. Tech.fortune.cmm.com/2012/08/09/the-worlds-most-popular-way-to-get-around/
3. www.goinggreentoday.com/blog/7-ways-that-bicycling-can-save-the-enviorment/
4. www.acdc.com/us/theband
5. www.Zootsports.com/about
6. National Bicycle Dealers Association.com
7. www.pearsoncycles.co.uk/store/content/43/herit
8. www.bicycling.com/maintence/featured-stories/hallowed-ground-best-bike-shops
9. Koppscycle.net/articles/kopps-cycle-history-pg59.html
10. Meritbadge.org/wiki/index.php/cycling
11. Neboridge.com/articles/staff-ing135/
12. www.newmoonski.com/our_company/why-buy.html
13. www.sugarsbikeshop.comwhysugars/
14. www.bucksbikes.com/
15. www.sierrabicycleworks.com
16. www.cedarbluffcycles.net/articles/mission-statement-pg101.html
17. www.riverfrontcycle.com
18. Scott-2013-Scott bikes and accessories catalog
19. www.sram.com/copying/about
20. www.speaktospoerle.com
21. www.hammernutrition.com
22. Retail.about.com/od/marketingsalespromotion/qt/product-knowledg.html
23. www.neboridge.com
24. Moots-2012 product catalog
25. Cannondale-2013 product catalog
26. www.sidiamerica.com/sidi/about.html

27. The Starbucks Experience, Joseph A. Michelli—the McGraw Hill Company 2007
28. http://articles.latimes.com/2012/aug/15/business/la-fi-home-improvement-2012081529. http://travel.spotcoolstuff.com/bicycle-store-travel/worlds-best-bicycle-shops
29. http://www.roadbikeaction.com/industry-insight/content/83/92/andy-ording.html
30. www.washingtonpost.com/blogs/on-small-business/post/how-to-breed-innovation-in-side-a-small-business
31. http://plus.google.com/104232795772550982787/about/hl=en
32. http://plus.google.com/100008371815345043026/about/hl=en

# RECOMMENDED READING

The Starbucks Experience - By Joseph Michelli
The Amazement Revolution - By Shep Hyken
Goals - By Brian Tracy
Write Fearlessly - By Jim Denney
Mojo - By Marshall Goldsmith
How to Be Like Walt - By Pat Williams
Creating Magic - By Lee Cockerell
The Encore Effect - By Mark Sanborn
Step Up and Play Big - By Chris Ruisi
The Cult of the Customer - By Shep Hyken
UP! Your Service! Great Ideas - By Ron Kaufman
Extreme Dreams Depend On Teams - By Pat Williams
The Zappos Experience - By Joseph Michelli

If you would like to contact Jim, or line up a speaking engagement. Please contact him here.
Jim@JimSerger.com
or visit www.jimserger.com

# ABOUT RED BIKE PUBLISHING

Our company is registered as a government contractor company with the CCR and VetBiz (DUNS 826859691). Specifically we are a service disabled veteran owned small business. Red Bike Publishing provides high quality books and include the following which can be found at www.redbikepublishing.com and Amazon.com:

PUBLISHING
Get Rich in a Niche-The Insider's Guide to Self-Publishing in a Specialized Industry ISBN: 978-1-936800-04-9

OTHER TOPICS
1. Rainy Street Stories-Reflections on Secret Wars, Espionage and Terrorism ISBN: 978-1-936800-10-0
2. 2000 Miles On Wisdom ISBN: 978-1-936800-20-9

NOVELS
Commitment-A Novel ASIN: B0057U3GLS

NATIONAL SECURITY TOPICS
1. DoD Security Clearances and Contracts Guidebook ISBN 978-1-936800-80-3 and ISBN 978-1-936800-99-5
2. Insider's Guide to Security Clearances ISBN: 9781936800988
3. ISP Certification-The Industrial Security Professional Exam Manual ISBN: 9780981620602
4. National Industrial Security Program Operating Manual (NISPOM) ISBN: 978098162060857
5. International Traffic in Arms Regulation (ITAR) ISBN: 97809816288

ARMY TOPICS
1. Ranger Handbook SH 21-76 ISBN-13: 978-1936800087
2. US Army Physical Readiness Training TC 3.22-20 ISBN:97809816240
3. US Army Physical Fitness Training FM 21-20 ISBN:97809816240

4. US Army Leadership FM 6-22 ISBN: 978-0981620671
5. US Army Drill and Ceremonies FM 3-21.5 ISBN: 978-1936800025

www.ingramcontent.com/pod-product-compliance
Lightning Source LLC
Chambersburg PA
CBHW070049100426
42734CB00040B/2803